Another Day

Previous to a return to parish life in the Diocese
of Bath and Wells in 1976, John Carden had
served the Church overseas in a number of
different capacities; as a missionary priest; as a
regional secretary based in Pakistan; and then as
Asia Secretary of the Church Missionary Society.
During this time he wrote *Empty Shoes*, a book of
meditations on Pakistan, and compiled *Morning
Noon and Night*, a collection of prayers from the
Third World. In 1984 he was licenced as a priest
in the Diocese of Jerusalem and took a short term
assignment with the Church of the Redeemer in
Amman. It was in Jordan – 'geographically and
spiritually very close to where it all began' – that
this second collection of prayers and meditations
was completed. He is currently working with the
World Council of Churches in Geneva.

Another Day

Prayers of the Human Family

John Carden

First published 1986
Triangle/SPCK
Holy Trinity Church
Marylebone Road
London NW1 4DU

British Library Cataloguing in Publication Data

Carden, John
    Another day: prayers of the human family.
    1. Prayer-books
    I. Title
    242'.8   BV245
    ISBN 0-281-04251-9

Filmset, printed and bound in Great Britain by
Hazell Watson & Viney Limited,
Member of the BPCC Group,
Aylesbury, Bucks

Contents

Introduction

'Prayer,' said the wayside pulpit outside the Chepstow chapel, 'is the key to the morning, the bolt at night.' Certainly it is that, and indeed all that falls between those two much-loved Collects, 'Almighty and most merciful God, who has safely brought us to the beginning of this day . . .', and 'Lighten our darkness . . .'

Having lived for a number of years in Pakistan, followed by wider experience of churches in Asia and the Middle East; then some years spent in an English parish the other side of the river from Chepstow, and now living and working in Jordan, the image of bolting a door at night and opening it again at the beginning of a new day has been illuminated for me by these different places and experiences.

From early morning waking until going to sleep at night the meditations and prayers in *Another Day* cover a similar range of needs and aspirations to those contained in an earlier collection, *Morning, Noon and Night*. As far as the choice of the subjects of the prayers is concerned, the sources from which they are drawn, and the comments that accompany them, this is a more informal and more personal book than the earlier one. Indeed, over the course of time I have come to see this as more of a devotional diary than a collection of prayers for widespread use.

Some of the prayers learned from those of other faiths are very much in this category, and perhaps belong properly to personal devotion, or to interfaith occasions, depending on individual inclination. Others, however, are of a limited application in a different sense; and will be difficult for most of us to identify with directly: that of the camel driver in the Sahel for instance, or the fishermen of Tanzania, or the prayer of that African tribesman, so hungry, that he asks God for even a very small polecat for a meal; or that of Christians in Central America whose prayers are for better lavatories. But even such prayers as these will all shed light on the things that are of vital concern and importance to other members of the human family and therefore rightly form the subject of their prayers and of our concern.

There are still many countries in the world where minorities find it difficult to sleep safely in their beds at night, or where doors are hammered on in the early hours. And in most countries in the west there are cities in which people – especially women – fear to go out alone after dusk, or even by day. So, if such prayers outweigh the rest at certain points, that is just how it is.

Very few of the prayers included here appeared in *Morning, Noon and Night* and most come from what we have now learned to call 'the two thirds world'. However, Pope Gregory's advice to Augustine to the effect that 'Good things are not to be loved because of place, but place because of good things' has been the guiding rule in this present selection, and it also includes a number of prayers which started life in my own country, and which have now come back via Africa and Asia loaded with new significance and richness. Translated into other languages and used in other contexts, these prayers have become so much part of the life and worship of so many people, that it now almost appears as if they had written them themselves.

Amidst such an abundance of riches the role of the compiler has been an easy and exciting one; and my search for prayers and meditations has followed naturally from membership of the Church Universal, and the need to exercise some kind of responsibility for care and prayer across the world. The task of typing and editing the prayers has been a harder one; and thanks are due to Joanne Lotreck of Connecticut, USA, but in Amman at the right time, for typing; and to the staff of SPCK for editing and obtaining permission for the use of the prayers in this book. I make no apologies for using these prayers personally, but if in the course of making them available to a wider circle I have neglected to acknowledge the origins of any of them, or have distorted their meanings, I beg the pardon of those who created them in the first place.

Amman   JOHN CARDEN
Hashemite Kingdom of Jordan,
1986

Safely to the beginning

Almighty and everlasting Father, we thank you that you
have brought us safely to the beginning of this day. Keep
us from falling into sin or running into danger; order us
in all our doings; and guide us to do always what is right
in your eyes; through Jesus Christ our Lord.

The Third Collect, for Grace: Alternative Service Book

Nobody knows for sure the particular circumstances in
which the Prayer Book Collects first came to be written and
used, except that in many cases they emerged in days when
keys and bolts were not just words to catch the eye and
kindle the imagination, but stern necessities of everyday
life. Days when the locksmith was, literally, a key figure in
every community, and men looked to his skill to provide
them with the security they needed in days of darkness
and lawlessness; the safe stronghold from which they might
emerge on ventures and enterprises of many different
kinds. This is still true of a large number of countries and
situations in our contemporary world.

As far as is known, the Collect for Grace, used in the
Order for Morning Prayer in the Anglican Church, first saw
the light of day in the early morning monastic office of
Prime, one of that series of services designed to punctuate
each day's events – whether good or bad – with frequent
assurances of God's presence and forgiveness, and the recollection of his redemptive acts.

This particular Collect seems to have been drawn from
what might be described as an old anthology of prayers
known as Alcuin's Sacramentary – an order of prayer col-
lated by a remarkable English scholar of the eighth century.

On Emperor Charlemagne's insistence, Alcuin of York's task was to bring some kind of order into the liturgical disarray of very confused times. It was out of this situation, and with a real feeling for the warmth and colour of words, a sensitivity to the varied emotional needs of men, and with Alcuin's English facility for compromise, that this Collect for Grace emerged, composed most probably from fragments – passionate fragments – from older times, and reflecting a human preoccupation with early morning moods and fears and apprehensions which goes back to the beginning of history.

Although our need of God's protection will be of a different order from those days, morning is still a time when keys are turned to open doors; when the postman comes bearing bad, or good news; when there is a hospital appointment to be kept, a wearing journey to be undertaken, a difficult meeting to be attended, a hard decision to be made, or new people to be met.

'If only we could listen to the words that men have used from the first dawning of day through to the falling of darkness, what a confusion and babble of voices would reach our ears . . .' writes Richard Harries. 'As the day begins, so words begin,' he says. 'First sleepy words, mumbled words, perhaps grunty grumbly words.' And 'as the day gathers pace, so words gather pace. Last minute things to say before leaving the house, things to remember on the way, things to say as soon as one arrives; words to tell, remind, inform, exhort' . . . Words to use in anger, to express intense emotion, to evoke solemnity . . . 'Words, words, words, all over the world a torrent of words.' This applies likewise to the words human beings have used to address the deity in every conceivable circumstance, ever since, as Genesis tells us, 'man first began to call upon God' (Genesis 4.26).

Many of the experiences embodied in the prayers that follow will be capable of wide application. Others, however, are one-off and very local. The sharp particularity, for instance, of the Nebraskan farmer's request may not commend itself even to his fellow farmer on the next-door ranch; while to hear God addressed in West African terms as the one who has the yam and the knife, and is requested to 'cut us a piece', is not likely to do much for a fellow Christian in rural Somerset whose principal diet is C of E Matins! These and a good many other instances of local prayer found in this book will convey a flavour of the wide variety of experience and need within God's family. Indeed, prayer seen in this way can provide a deep experience of human solidarity even though its forms are sharply particular, and, as Bishop Cragg quotes somewhere, can be the means of facilitating 'a sort of devotional "transmigration" of soul into the lives of peasants, sailors, factory hands and rulers . . .' and so on. Hence the inclusion in this collection, of the Radiating Prayer in the section 'Good Morning', and the prayers on the theme of 'One World'.

So, thinking of my colleagues in the Episcopal Church of Jerusalem and the Middle East, what better words, I ask myself, to put into incomparable Arabic, and to say over the Christians of this troubled part of the world, than these?

Or, much thumbed and prayed over hundreds of prayer-desks in Indian and Pakistani and African churches, what better words can local pastors find than ones which ask for God's protection and sustenance for their needy people for just one day at a time?

Or, in the more familiar setting of most First World countries where medical and other forms of care are assured from beginning to end of life, what more appropriate words may be found than these with which to address the loneliness and pain of much of our lives? What do you say, for instance, to that person who can no longer go on living alone in her own home, but must move elsewhere to a place where there are few familiar faces or belongings, and who is confronted with an endless succession of days and years ahead confined to an impersonal room and among unfamiliar people? In these circumstances what is there to say unless it be along the lines suggested by this Collect, that God brings us safely to the beginning of each new day, not just allowing it to happen, but actually himself leading us to it? That life isn't just an endless succession of days that 'just happen', but that God personally and lovingly gives us the new day and promises to be with us in it?

Or, further afield, what is one to say and ask for those imprisoned in countries with highly restrictive regimes, except to pray that they may find some way of marking the days; gain some access to a calendar; find some form of daily reading? That they may sometimes catch a glimpse of a clock, or of the rising or setting sun, so that one day may not merge into the next in a way which might suggest that the passing of days is of no account to God either?

In certain moods and in certain circumstances the words 'another day' are leaden words, and are frequently said with little enthusiasm. We all experience such moods from time to time; and such occasions and times are provided for in some of the prayers that follow, especially those arising out of specific situations, and said on behalf of those who have special reason to dread the arrival of a new day. But the very word 'God' used in so many of the prayers is, as some-one has said, a beckoning word, and at no point is that beckoning more evident than in the words of those morning prayers which enable us to respond to the prospect of 'another day' with anticipation and trust.

Opening our eyes

1

Lord! Give us weak eyes for things which are of no account and clear eyes for all Thy truth.

Sören Kierkegaard. Quoted at the beginning of a Japanese work of Christian theology

2

Strengthen, O Lord, our weakness in Thy compassion, and comfort and help the wants of our soul in Thy loving kindness. Waken our thoughts from sleep, and lighten the weight of our limbs; wash us and cleanse us from the filth of our sins.

Enlighten the darkness of our minds, stretch forth Thy helping hand, confirm and give us strength; that we may arise and confess Thee and glorify Thee without ceasing all the days of our life, O Lord of all.

Nestorian Liturgy

3

Holy Father,
In the wisdom of Thy Perfection
Help me to understand my imperfection.

Prayer from Egypt

4

Lord God most high, may we offer Thee praise and thankfulness for Thy loving kindness in letting us hear about Thy precious Gospel. We are happy to be called Christians, and so make us all real ones. Grant us the power to feel Thy presence among us. Cleanse our hearts and make them clear like crystals in order that we may see Thee and that the Holy Spirit may dwell in us. Dear Lord . . . there are many friends of ours who have not heard about Thy precious name nor have they seen Thy light. Help us all to dedicate ourselves more in Thy service and to shine for Thee. Forgive us for being selfish and letting Thy light grow dim. We ask these things in the name of the Great Lord, Jesus Christ whose merits lift us from sin.

Thai woman

5

Your idol is shattered in the dust to prove that God's dust is greater than your idol.

Rabindranath Tagore, Bengali poet

6

Lord, who are merciful as well as just
Incline Thine ear, to me, a child of dust
Not what I would, O Lord, I offer Thee
Alas! but what I can.

Father Almighty, who has made me man,
and bade me look to heav'n, for Thou art there,
Accept my sacrifice and humble prayer:
Four things, which are in Thy treasury,
I lay before Thee, Lord, with this petition:
My nothingness, my wants, my sin, and my contrition.

Persian prayer; translated by Robert Southey

7

No one can put together what has crumbled into dust,
but you can restore a conscience turned to ashes;
you can restore to its former beauty a soul lost and
    without hope.

With you, there is nothing that cannot be redeemed;
you are love, you are creator and redeemer;
we praise you, singing: Alleluia!

> From the prayers and poems of Fr. Gregory Petrov, Russian
> Orthodox protopriest, who suffered imprisonment during Sta-
> lin's purges of the 1930s and composed in prison, just before
> he died in the early 1940s.

8

My heart is lit
by strange flames
and its withered grasses
crackle in their heat.
The winds of passion
blow through the dead branches
of its leafless trees
blazing an ocherous trail
for strange flames
that leap and dance
with fiendish glee
in my heart.

I burn, O Lord,
for strange flames
lick with devouring tongues
at all that grows
within my heart.
Save me, O Lord,
from these raging fires
that consume my inmost being.
Send down Thy heavenly rain
of tender mercy,
wet me through and through
with Thy torrential love
till every strange flame
is banished for ever
from my scorched heart.

Chandran Devanesen, Indian Christian

9

O God, pull out of my heart all the weeds and the dry grass and let each hollow be filled with thine own self.

Mexican peasant

10

As our tropical sun gives forth its light, so let the rays from thy face enter every nook of my being and drive away all darkness within.

Prayer from the Philippines

11

O my God, how gentle art Thou with him who has transgressed against Thee, how near Thou art to him who seeks Thee, how tender to him who petitions Thee, how kindly to him who hopes in Thee. By what is hidden of Thy Names and by what the veils conceal of Thy splendour, forgive this restless spirit, this anguished heart.

Sufi prayer

12

You make one leetle prayer. You say: 'Le bon Fadder, oh! I want to come back, I so tire, so hungree; so sorree.

Prayer of French Canadian, from *Black Rock* by Ralph Connor

13

O God of Abraham, God of Isaac, and God of Jacob, the beginning and the end; without you we can do nothing. The great river is not big enough for you to wash your hands in. You have the yam and you have the knife; we cannot eat unless you cut us a piece. We are like ants in your sight. We are little children who only wash their stomach when they bath, leaving their back dry.

Prayer from West Africa, from *No Longer at Ease* by Chinua Achebe

I am only a spark
Make me a fire.
I am only a string
Make me a lyre.
I am only a drop
Make me a fountain.
I am only an ant hill
Make me a mountain.
I am only a feather
Make me a wing.
I am only a rag
Make me a King!

Prayer from Mexico

15

We are the scars on Thy person. Just as a man cannot throw away a scar on his body, so Thou canst not easily rid Thyself of us. Help us to know the wonder of this truth, so that we may truly serve Thee.

Prayer from Nigeria

16

Lord, Thou knowest that I am a hundred times worse than Thou hast declared. But beyond my exertion and action, beyond good and evil, faith and infidelity, beyond living righteously or behaving disobediently, I had great hope of Thy loving kindness. I turn again to that pure grace. I do not regard my own works. Thou gavest me my being as a robe of honour: I have always relied on that munificence.

Sufi prayer

17

Grant us, O Lord, in our coming and our going, in our staying, in the things we speak, and will, and ponder, to be immune from doubts and notions and illusions which shroud our heart from exploring the hidden mysteries.

Sufi prayer

18

Lord, help me never to use my reason against the Truth.

Jewish prayer

19

Eternal and gracious Father, in the darkness and uncertainty of life our minds reach upwards to know you, flitting here and there, beckoned on by any shaft of brightness which promises to lead us to your eternal light. But we soon miss the trail and our eyes soon get accustomed to the rays; they become shuttered and we give up the search, content to follow what, in our self-imposed blindness, we think produces the light which breaks upon our shuttered eyelids. Father, guide our path, direct our flight, teach us how to open our eyes, steady our gaze and fix our eyes only on your eternal being, that we may never be distracted by the shady rests along the road but press onwards and upwards along the path you show us.

Through your only Son Jesus Christ teach us how to follow you; make firm our faltering slippery grip, and make us to desire the joy and excitement of following above the passing and illusive pleasure of finding, that so we may spend all our days in glad obedience and joyful submission as your dear children.

Bishop Prince Thompson, Freetown, Sierra Leone

20

From the unreal lead me to the real
from darkness lead me to light
from death lead me to immortality.

From the Brhad-aranyaka Upanishad, this has been further

adapted by Satish Kumar and adopted by the teachers of many faiths as the Universal Prayer for Peace, as follows:

Lead me from Death to Life
　　from Falsehood to Truth
Lead me from Despair to Hope
　　from Fear to Trust
Lead me from Hate to Love
　　from War to Peace
Let Peace fill our Heart
　　our World, our Universe.
Peace　Peace　Peace

21

O God, show us all things in this house of deception: show them as they really are.

Sufi prayer

22

Lord, save me from self-vindication.

Attributed to St Augustine of Hippo (354–430)

23

'I was very late arriving yesterday for a special harvest service which I'd promised to attend,' reflects a European missionary in West Africa, 'and subsequently remarked to the pastor that he must have thought I'd broken my promise. Immediately he replied, "No; Europeans always keep their promises." '

Searching words, that led to the following self-examination:

'Europeans always keep their promises.' Do they? Do I?
Oh yes, I will arrive at the agreed place
at the agreed time (more or less)
even for the agreed purpose.
But the *ethos* behind the purpose?
The *meaning* inside the agreement?

My promise to follow, for example –
to follow the Man, the God of integrity and of love
    – there's not much love
in keeping of my promises
    – there's not much caring
in the execution of my agreements
    – and little integrity
in the carrying out of my resolutions.

Instead, a routine keeping of the letter
not the spirit, of the promise.

Perhaps the promised Spirit would assist.

'Europeans keep their promises.'
Do I? Do you? Does God?

Elizabeth Leicester, CMS mission partner, Nigeria: a European
act of self-examination prior to Pentecost.

24

Thank you, Lord, for knowing me better than I know
myself, and for letting me know myself better than others
know me. Make me better than they suppose, and forgive
me for what they do not know.

> Abu Bekr, father-in-law of Mohammed and first Muslim
> Khalif, 572–634, is said to have recited this prayer when he
> heard people praising him.

25

When we are strong enough to stop telling the Big Lie, O
God, give us even more courage to stop telling the little
smooth lies.

Prayer from Hawaii

26

God, first among all spirits
Supreme being who feels something for us
You, Possessor of all, who have inner peace

You, who are the same outside and inside
Be our Creator, give us wisdom and strength
So that we may grow to be sincere and true.
And, you, God, Master of everything
Grant us your help to live for others
So that we may live for you.

Ancient African prayer

27

Lord, PREPARE us to be honest when we articulate our Christian beliefs to persons of other faiths;

Lord, HELP us to be honest when we include personal emotions in expressing our religious experiences;

Lord, SUBMIT us to be honest when we respond to our mission to bear your cross;

Lord, TRANSFORM us to be honest when we contradict our Christian values and simplicity;

Lord, GUARD us to be honest to the virtue of humility when we become popular in a community;

Lord, CREATE us to be honest in the rays of your love, grace and power;

Lord, PENETRATE us to be honest when we partake at your supper;

Lord, TRANSMIT us to be honest when we associate sectarian Christianity with St Paul's emphasis on Justification by Faith;

Lord, ESTABLISH us to be honest and true to thy Word and help us to refrain from indulging in unfruitful controversies;

Lord, EQUIP us to be honest when we undertake serious commitments in your Church;

Lord, LIBERATE us to be honest when we find our freedom from the bondage of sectarian teachings;

Lord, RESTORE us to be honest when we realise the significance of Christian challenges;

Lord, RECONCILE us to be honest in our service to the drug addicts, downtrodden, jobless and helpless;

Lord, ACTIVATE us to be honest in the act of charity;
Lord, PRESERVE us to be honest when we confess our
Creed and faith in the Church;
Lord, MOULD us to be honest when we present ourselves
at the table in your Kingdom.

Solomon Rajah, Malaysia

28

Loving God, whose glory outshines the sun, open our lives
to the inspiration of your Holy Spirit that we may fully
reflect the glory of your love and share ourselves with one
another in this time of . . . In Christ's name we pray.
Amen.

Opening prayer to be used before an act of common worship,
intercession or study; written for the 6th Assembly of the World
Council of Churches, Vancouver.

Thou, God

29

There can be all the difference in the world between beginning a prayer with 'O Almighty God' and beginning it with 'Thou' breathed to Someone – there. We need to practise that, until the Presence becomes so real that He is in deed and in truth possessing the very centre where for us the important 'I' stands so supreme.

Florence Allshorn of Uganda and St Julian's, England

30

To Him of Whom one cannot speak
      to Him one must pray.

Ludwig Wittgenstein. Adapted by Viktor E. Frankl, psychiatrist and concentration camp survivor

31

O God, grant that we may never speak to you from the mind and with the lips, without at the same time addressing you – God – in the heart. So be it.

Donald Nicholl, of the Ecumenical Institute, Tantur, near Bethlehem, and Selly Oak Colleges, Birmingham.

32

Some time ago a poor young Indian girl lay seriously ill in a Calcutta hospital. She knew that she was not likely to recover, but she was not afraid. One afternoon she had lain quite still, with her eyes shut, and for so long that the nurse came to see if she was all right. The girl opened her eyes. Had she been asleep? asked the nurse. 'No,' said the girl, 'I was praying.' 'What were you asking God for, to make you well?' asked the nurse. 'No, I wasn't asking for anything. I was just loving him.'

> 'It is in such quiet, deep communion with God' wrote Philip Loyd, then Bishop of Nasik, 'that spiritual forces beyond our reckoning or comprehension are released. They can be released in and through us, if we will only draw near to him prepared, expectant, waiting to love him.'

33

O my God, I invoke Thee in public as lords are invoked, but in private as loved ones are invoked. Publicly I say, 'O my God!' but privately I say, 'O my Beloved!'

Sufi mystic

34

O Lord, grant us to love Thee; grant that we may love those that love Thee; grant that we may do the deeds that win Thy love. Make the love of Thee to be dearer to us than ourselves, than our families, than wealth, and even than cool water.

Prayer of Mohammed

35

Please, O Lord, let the fiery honeyed force of your love lap up my spirit from everything that is under Heaven: so that I may die for love of love for you, who deigned to die for love of love of me.

Prayer attributed to St Francis by the Franciscan Custody of the Holy Land

36

Increase me, O Lord,
     in marvelling at Thee

Shaikh Admad Al'Alawi, 20th-century Sufi saint of Tunisia

37

O great God, who art Thou? Where art Thou? Show Thyself to me!

Daily prayer of Venkayya, outcaste convert, the Church of South
India; offered every day for three years

38

Teach me to pray – thus help me to bore a hole through
which I can see Thee.

Prayer from New Guinea

39

O God! Whatever share of this world Thou hast allotted to
me, bestow it on Thine enemies; and whatever share of
the next world Thou has allotted to me, bestow it on Thy
friends. Thou art enough for me.

Rabi'ah of Basra, Muslim mystic

40

O God, I call upon Thee by Thy entire glory, by Thy beauty
at its most beautiful . . . all things suppliant unto Thee are
beloved of Thee: so, O God, I call upon Thee by all things
suppliant unto Thee. O God, I call upon Thee by that which
Thou art, in power and in greatness, calling upon Thee by
every several element of that power and majesty. I see Thee
thus, O God, in the name of that wherewith Thou answerest
when I call upon Thee. Our desire is unto Thee, O God,
Thine are the Names most excellent and the attributes most
high. Thine is the supremacy, the glory and the grace.

Sufi prayer

41

O God, who art the unsearchable abyss of peace, the ineffable sea of love, the fountain of blessings and the bestower of affection, who sendest peace to those that receive it; Open to us this day the sea of Thy love and water us with plenteous streams from the riches of Thy grace and from the most sweet springs of Thy kindness. Make us children of quietness and heirs of peace, enkindle in us the fire of Thy love; sow in us Thy fear; strengthen our weakness by Thy power; bind us closely to Thee and to each other in our firm and indissoluble bond of unity.

Syrian Clementine Liturgy

42

Ah, Lord our God, if Thou art so lovely in Thy creatures, how exceedingly beautiful and ravishing Thou must be in Thyself!

Blessed Henry Suso, 1300–1366

43

Watching a marvellous film
about the ocean depths
I felt a huge desire
to help the fish
understand how lucky they are
to live immersed
in so much splendour.
Imagine then my thirst
to cry to men, my brothers,
that we lived immersed –
coming and going,
swimming to and fro –
not in the oceans
but in God himself.

Archbishop Dom Helda Camara, Brazil

44

Give us this day our daily discovery.

The former Archbishop of Canterbury, Dr Donald Coggan, speaking at a Church of South India Synod on the necessity of Christians maintaining a propensity for surprise and wonder, prompted in one delegate the recollection of this prayer often used by the Quaker, Dr Rendell Harris.

Good morning

45

Life is beginning to stir. What will the day be like?

Anatoli Levitin, persecuted Russian Orthodox Christian

46

O Lord, our heavenly Father, Almighty and everlasting God, who hast safely brought us to the beginning of this day: Defend us in the same with thy mighty power; and grant that this day we fall into no sin, neither run into any kind of danger; but that all our doings may be ordered by thy governance, to do always that is righteous in thy sight; through Jesus Christ our Lord. Amen.

Book of Common Prayer

47

This day is dear to me above all other days for today the Beloved Lord is a guest in my house.

Kabir, 15th-century North Indian mystic and poet

Kabir was born, probably in Benares, about the year 1441. He spent the greater part of his life working as a humble weaver in his native city, and there composed his mystical poetry; he probably died about 1518.

48

O Christ, we come into Thy presence, and how beautiful it is! There is no place so beautiful as the place where Thou art.

Another prayer from India

49

O God and Lord, this flesh and body of mine are the threshold of Thy door, wherein I have slept and squatted, I am before Thee, and I will not go from Thy presence to any other place. This body of mine, O God, is Thy workshop and my senses are engraved by Thee.

I have placed them before Thee: whatever Thou wilt do Thou engrave upon them, O God. I have come before Thee, for Thou art my Lord: whom have I but Thee? If I depart hence, O God, whither shall I go? What place have I where I may alight and dwell? For Thou art my Lord: I know no other to be my Lord, but Thee.

Sufi act of recollection

50

Father-Creator, Provider-from-of-old, Ancient-of-days – fresh-born from the womb of night are we. In the first dawning of the new day draw we nigh unto Thee. Forlorn are the eyes till they have seen the Chief.

Bushman's prayer, South Africa

51

Do not say 'It is morning' and dismiss it with a name of yesterday. See it for the first time as a new-born child that has no name.

Rabindranath Tagore

52

Thanks be to Thee, O Lord, for this gift of a new day, which seemeth to me so like other days, yet is indeed not like but different. It is Thy newest handiwork, the fruit of Thy longest patience. Make it for me a time for service and a time for loving.

John Hoyland, a prayer used in Calcutta

53

O God, receive us as Thy guests this morning.
Give to us before we leave.

African Christian

54

What a glorious morning!
The sun has not hid his beauty behind the misty sky.
The flowers are all full of freshness and vigour.
The birds are flying about from branch to branch
And in my mind there is a temporary calm.
I am not certain of the moment of its breakdown
It is so delicate –
I have not seen anything more delicate
Than my heart and my being.
The smallest mishap,
A look,
The absence of a letter,
The falling down of a book from the table
Can upset my equilibrium.

Is there no escape from this?

Yes, Christ is my refuge.
He is my calm.
And When I am in His hands,
I revel like a child in its mother's arms.

M. A. Thomas, Indian Christian

55

O Master, Lord, God Almighty, Father of our Lord, our
God, our Saviour Jesus Christ, we thank Thee upon every
condition, for any condition and in whatever condition. For
Thou hast covered us, supported us, preserved us, accepted
us unto Thee, had compassion on us, sustained us and
brought us into this hour. Wherefore we pray and entreat
Thy goodness, O lover-of-mankind, grant us to complete

this holy day and all the days of our life in all peace with
Thy fear.

Thanksgiving Prayer: Coptic Orthodox Liturgy

56

Lord, help me to remember that nothing is going to happen
today that you and I cannot handle together.

Prayer used by Saidie Patterson, peace-maker, Shankhill, Northern Ireland

> This idea of co-operation between the human and the divine
> in surmounting impossible obstacles is probably a universal one.

57

The day is there.
There is the sun.
Ships are in the harbour,
But is there work for me?
The others have friends.
They also have money.
They have given a dash of whisky.
And I stand aside
and have no work.
Can't you make work for me
in the harbour,
dear Lord,
so that I can share money
with my wife and children?
Then, on Sunday,
I can put something in the plate.
Please let me have work.
Dear Lord Jesus,
we praise you.   Amen

Prayer from West Africa: 'Please let me have work.'

> In view of widespread under-employment in so many countries
> it seems strange that there are so few prayers written on this
> subject.

Lord, grant me to meet with tranquillity of soul all that may befall me this day. Grant that I may obey Thy holy will every hour of this day; guide me and maintain me in all things, reveal to me Thy will for me and those about me. Whatever news I may receive this day, grant that I may accept it with a tranquil soul and in the firm conviction of Thy holy will in all things. In all my words and deeds, guide my thoughts and emotions, in all unforeseen circumstances let me not forget that all these things are permitted by Thee.

Teach me, O Lord, to deal openly and wisely with all, in the community, in my own family . . . causing grief or embarrassment to no one, but comforting, aiding and counselling all.

Lord, grant me the strength to bear the weariness of the coming day, and all the events that occur in the course of the day.

Guide my will and teach me, O Lord, to pray to Thee, to believe, hope, endure patiently, forgive and love.

Russian Christian

Open your doors of mercy, Lord:
hear our prayer and have mercy upon our souls.
Lord of the morning and ruler of the seasons:
hear our prayer and have mercy upon our souls.
Shine on us Lord, and make us light like the day:
let your light shine in our minds and drive away the
    shadows of error and night.
The creation is full of light, give your light also to our
    hearts:
that we may praise you all the day long.
The morning and evening praise you, Lord:
they bring you the prayers of your Church.

Light which gives light to all creatures:
give light to our minds that we may thank you, Lord.

Syrian Orthodox Church

60

Dear Jesus, help us to spread your fragrance everywhere
we go.
Flood our souls with your spirit and life.
Penetrate and possess our whole being so utterly that our
lives may only be a radiance of yours.
Shine through us, and be so in us, that every soul we
come in contact with may feel your presence in our
soul.
Let them look up and see no longer us but only Jesus!
Stay with us, and then we shall begin to shine as you
shine; so to share as to be a light to others; the light O
Jesus, will be all from you, none of it will be ours; it
will be you, shining on others through us.
Let us preach you without preaching, not by words but
by our example, by the catching force, the sympathetic
influence of what we do, the evident fullness of the love
our hearts bear to you.

Cardinal Newman. (1801–90): used daily by Mother Teresa's
Missionaries of Charity

61

You grant me the clear confidence that You exist, and that
You will ensure that not all the ways of goodness are
blocked.

Alexander Solzhenitsyn

62

Show to all creatures love, and you will be happy, for when
you love all things, you love the Lord, for He is all in all.

Tulsi Das, Indian poet

63

Blessed be Thou, O God – my Father, his Father, her Father, their Father, our Father.

64

Beginning from within the heart, and sending out to those
near to us, then in widening circles to others
in our village or town,
to those of our own nation,
then neighbouring nations,
till finally the whole of mankind, living and
departed, is reached in the radiation of good will,
compassion, love, joy, peace, blessing,
remembering that these lovely dispositions start
from God within ourselves and are reinforced by His
infinitely more generous radiation.

The Radiating Prayer

With reference to this pattern of prayer, George Appleton writes in his *One man's prayers*, 'There is in Buddhism a lovely devotional practice in which the devout Buddhist sits in quiet meditation and radiates to all living beings, love, joy, compassion, and peace in turn. The spirit of this practice is expressed in the following Buddhist 'prayer' or aspiration:

Now may every living thing, young and old, weak or strong, living near or far, known or unknown, living or departed or yet unborn, may every living thing be full of bliss.

He goes on to make the point that while for many Buddhists the practice of these noble exercises would be a humanistic one, nevertheless Christians may use them in a framework of their belief in God-in-Christ, offering themselves thus as a channel for his universal love, and adding their own small contribution of love, joy, compassion and peace to God's infinitely more generous radiation.

The open door

65

Many a song have I sung in many a mood of mind,
but their notes have always proclaimed:
    He comes, comes, ever comes.

                          Rabindranath Tagore

66

Lord, grant that I may open the door of my mind to be
taught, and the gate of my heart to be warmed by Thy love.

67

O God, I knock at the door of thy mercy with the hand of
my hope.

                                     Sufi prayer

68

When the heart is hard and parched, come upon me with a
shower of mercy. When grace is lost from life, come with
a burst of song. When tumultuous work raises its din on all
sides, shutting me out from beyond, come to me, my Lord
of silence, with Thy peace and rest. When my beggarly
heart sits crouched, shut up in a corner, break open the
door, my King, and come with the ceremony of a king.

                          Rabindranath Tagore

69

Lord, oil the hinges of our hearts' doors that they may
swing gently and easily to welcome your coming.

A New Guinea Christian describes Advent in this way: 'At
Advent, we should try the key to our heart's door. It may have

gathered rust. If so, this is the time to oil it, in order that the heart's door may open more easily when the Lord Jesus wants to enter at Christmas time.'

70

Put your ear to the ground
and identify the noises round you.
Predominant are
anxious, restless footsteps,
frightened footsteps in the dark,
footsteps bitter and rebellious.
No sound as yet
of hope's first footsteps.
Glue your ear to the ground again.
Hold your breath.
Put out your advance antennae:
The Master is on his way.
Most likely he will not get here
when things are going well,
but in bad times
when the going's unsure and painful.

Archbishop Dom Helder Camara, Brazil

71

To find I must seek
Seek, and not improvise, or imitate
Seek, and not beg, borrow or steal
I must leave the ninety and nine I have
And seek after the one I want
I must light the candle that I have
Not wait for the searchlight I do not have
I must bend down and sweep every corner
Not just the tidy places; but all the dark crannies
I must seek desperately as Hagar did
Searching for water in the wilderness
Yes, like the hart that panteth after the water brook
I must seek early in the morning and late at night

As the maiden seeking him for whom her soul does long
I must seek with passion as did young Saul of Tarsus
I must seek with caution as did old Nicodemus
I must seek in the crowd as did the man Zacchaeus
I must seek alone as did Mary of Magdala
I must seek with stubborn doubts as Thomas did
I must seek with faith for the city I have not seen
I must seek with faith, with hope, with love
I must seek in despair, in doubt and in anguish
But to find I must *seek*.

To open, I must knock
Knock, and not just vaguely feel
Knock, and not just gently tap
I must knock as the widow did at the door of the callous
    judge
I must knock as the man did at the door of his sleeping
    friend.
I must knock at the door
Not with my tiny finger
Not with my unsure hand
But with my hard and strong head
I must knock not once, or twice, or thrice
But till it hurts, and till I bleed
For when my thick skull bleeds
I will come to my senses
As did the son that ran away
And then I will know I was knocking
But knocking at the wrong door
And *then* I will find the open door.

A seeker in India

72

Jesus, Lord, for whom an inn could find no room, whom
thine own world would not receive, never let me close my
door against thee, nor against the least of my brethren in
their least need.

Stand not then at my door and knock, though that be a miracle of mercy, but lift the latch and enter, Jesus, Lord.

This prayer by Eric Milner-White is quoted by George Appleton in *Journey for a Soul*. What an incalculable debt the world of prayer and devotion owes to these two men.

73

Sometimes the book I'm reading falls from my hands and treasure-laden argosies of thought bear me across seas of purpling splendour.

Sometimes eternity spreads before me like a vast field of flowers where the years of my life seem like small boys chasing butterflies through meadow gateways of heaven.

Sometimes I gaze upon Thee in all Thy manifold beauty until I become oblivious of all else and time becomes a distant sense like the unconscious throbbing of a pulse.

Then comes the postman's knock. I greet him with a smile for his knock reminds me of the time of day, of births, deaths, and marriages, of the calendar of local events, of bitterness and sweetness, of joy and sorrow – all the alternating lights and shades of daily human history.

And then I know, O Lord, that the love I taste from Thee is the love that is in my love for others, and the love that others have for me.

Even as eternity is measured by Thy hands on a clock so is Thy love measured to us in the measure with which we love, until love speaks to perfect Love without fear.

Chandran Devanesen, India

Moving out

Today Lord
A new day
Laid open,
And here am I
Waiting to step into it
And yet there is a feeling of uncertainty
Even fear
Of what it holds
Fear of what it will demand of me
Have I the resources, Lord,
To meet this day?
Can I enter it
With joy and certainty and contentment?

My child,
This is the day I have made
For you
Accept it gladly
Dance into it
And carry with you
The joy of resurrection
The peace of self-giving
The love that forgives and gives
Delight yourself in this day
As a child delights
In all that is new
Revel in it
Absorb it
For it is TODAY, new
That day that I have made.

Myrtle Hall, working with mentally handicapped children in
Nigeria

75

Our Father in Heaven, I thank Thee that Thou has led me
into the Light. I thank Thee for sending the Saviour to call
me from death to life. I confess that I was dead in sin before
I heard His call, but when I heard Him, like Lazarus, I
arose. But, O my Father, the grave clothes bind me still.
Old habits that I cannot throw off, old customs that are so
much a part of my life that I am helpless to live the new life
that Christ calls me to live. Give me strength, O Father, to
break the bonds; give me courage to live a new life in Thee;
give me faith, to believe that with Thy help I cannot fail.
And this I ask in the Saviour's name who has taught me to
come to Thee. Amen

Prayer from Taiwan

76

Eternal Love, Father, Son, Holy Ghost, I believe in Thee.
I hope in Thy patient love.
I hope in Thy powerful love.
I hope in Thy purposeful love.
   O Love, I believe Thee, I Trust Thee.
   O Love, I desire Thee above all else.
   O Love, be true love within me, lest I fail Thee.

*Bishop Frank Weston of Zanzibar. Prayer of affirmation before
going outside*

77

And now dear God, what can I do for you?

English child

78

This is my prayer to Thee, my Lord. Give me the strength
to make my love fruitful in service.

Hindu prayer

My Lord, and my God:
Lord, it is enough for me of honour that I should be your
servant: it is enough for me of grace that you should be my
Lord.

Taharat al-Qulub. Translated by Constance Padwick

80

Dear Lord, let us start our work in faith, continue in obedience, and finish with love.

Prayer found in a church in the English Quantocks.

In that setting this prayer seems to epitomise the spirit of all
country churchgoing at its best.

81

Here I am, Lord – body, heart and soul. Grant that with
your love, I may be big enough to reach the world
And small enough to be at one with you.

Meditation of Mother Teresa of Calcutta, and used by her world-
wide Missionaries of Charity

82

O Lord,
May we be sandals under your feet,
wherever you want to go. Amen

Joe and Decie Church

Prayed as they knelt on the English moors, rededicating themselves to the service of Africa and the renewal of the Church
there.

83

The pews of your parish church,
The organ and the font
Will simply not fit

Into your air luggage.
You will have to leave behind also, I'm afraid,
The harvest supper, the historic tombs
And a lot of other clobber,
Irrelevancies that might have comforted you
When you arrived in Africa, the Far East,
Or wherever it is you are going.

For a journey into the undefined
The mind
Should not be overweight.
Travel light across the frontiers –
Your British passport will take you so far –
And no further.
And you must declare your luggage.
The mind's airbag containing
Western frames of thought, a little new theology,
Christian assumptions about men of other faiths,
Unexamined racial prejudice that perhaps, after all,
British is best;
An obsession with time, speed and punctuality;
A fear of snakes, unboiled water
And loss of identity;
Words, logic and a dislike of the inexact;
Along with a real desire to be useful, friendly
And somehow, as a Christian and British
To keep the flag flying.

This may exceed 44 lbs.

Much of your luggage is inevitable, of course,
And certainly not useless,
Provided you can see it for what it is
And can quickly reject what is secondary
If you have to bail out.
An overnight bag containing
Professional skill, goodwill,
An open mind and your integrity

34

Is all you need to cross the frontiers.
It really is advisable to travel light.

Uncluttered, you will see
Not only problems of administration,
Not only problems of your own survival,
But people.
Across the frontiers of the human face
In the silence where only a smile is articulate
You will touch and feel a fabric,
Woven in patterns similar and dissimilar to yours
Of light and shadow, beauty and despair,
Of wisdom, fear, stupidity and pain,
Human cloth, worn by men and women,
Warm with their life, bright with their truth.
Feel it and see
How they, like you, hunger and thirst,
How they would travel across your frontiers,
Sharing their bread,
Searching for water,
Would drink deep with you at the wells of God
The Names, the Nameless,
Inexpressible –
Love's hope,
Love's certainty,
Your mutual destination –
The end in the beginning,
The point of your departure.

USPG missionary: For a missionary packing

84

O send out Thy light and Thy truth, that I may live always
near to Thee, my God. Oh, let me feel Thy love, that I may
be, as it were, already in heaven, that I may do all my work
as the angels do theirs; and, oh, let me be ready for every
work, be ready to go out or go in, to stay or depart, just as
Thou shalt appoint. Lord, let me have no will of my own;

nor consider my true happiness as depending, in the smallest degree, on anything that can befall me outwardly, but as consisting altogether in conformity to Thy will.

> From the journals of Henry Martyn, 1781–1812, to which he confided his innermost thoughts and wistful letters. These are described by Bishop Kenneth Cragg as 'among the richest documents of personal discipleship and spiritual devotion'.

85

Great Spirit, you are everything,
and yet above everything.
You are first and always have been.

Through you our children will have strong hearts and they will walk the straight path in a sacred manner.

Help me to walk the sacred path of life without difficulty with my mind and heart continually fixed on you!
    Amen.

Lakota prayer. St Joseph's Indian School, Chamberlain, South Dakota

86

Lord, I am like a bicycle and my tyres are flat.
Blow me up, and then ride me!

African boy

87

Beat us, O our Father, not hard enough to give us great pain, but beat us a little, enough to make us travel in Thy path.

Prayer from the Sudan

88

We are bound for . . . smooth away the difficulties of the road for us, and give us sunlight.

Prayer from the Celebes

O Spirit, grant us a calm lake, little wind, little rain, so that the canoes may proceed well, so that they may proceed speedily.

Fisherman's Prayer, Tanzania

90

I am a man of little faith.
Every tide in life has passed away smoothly,
But I have forgotten that.
The giant tides that seem to rush against me
I am afraid will wash me away.
And I am crying like a little child,
Stretching out my hand for help.
Am I not a man of little faith?
The hand of my Master,
Who is the Lord of the seas,
Is around my shoulders.
In my fear and hurry,
I forget His grip
And look in vain for other help.
I am safe.

The tides have passed away like a dream.
But they threaten me again.
In my little boat,
With His hand upon my shoulders,
I shall play upon the tides,
Conquering them,
Enjoying the ever present company of my Master.

M. A. Thomas, India

91

Listen, O Lord of the meeting rivers,
Things standing shall fall
But the moving ever shall stay.

Basavanna, medieval saint of South India

92

In the Name of God be the
course and the mooring.

From the Qur'an. Prayer of Noah as he launched the ark, and of
Muslim pilgrims as they set out for Mecca.

93

The Lord bless thee, and keep thee;
the Lord make His face to shine upon thee,
and be gracious unto thee; the Lord turn His
face unto thee, and give thee peace. May it
be Thy will, Lord of Heaven and Earth, to
lead us to peace and safety, to fly us in peace
and safety to our desired destination to find
life, joy and peace. Guard and watch us who
fly the air routes and cross the seaways and
travel the overland passes. Make firm the
hands that guide the steering and sustain their
spirit, so that they may lead us in peace and
safety. For in You alone is our shelter from
now unto eternity. Amen

Jewish prayer for travellers

94

More prayers fly up over obstinate internal combustion
engines than over the pagan masses!

Uganda missionary

This is an exaggeration which probably does the missionaries
in question an injustice, but there is an element of truth in
the fact that transport; getting around; getting around safely;
communication; searching people out; following people up;
are very important, and do take up an inordinate amount of
time, and make heavy demands upon internal combustion
engines and their servicing.

Lord, turn our thought into a blessing for all who have trouble with cars.

JBC

95

God bless Africa.
Give her good roads and adequate transport and careful
    drivers.
Give her also a wise and compassionate economy so that
    food – the food of life – may reach every remotest part
    and that every person's need be met.
God bless Africa.

JBC

'We could bury Africa five feet deep in food; no problem at
all,' declared one United Nations official in a moment of exas-
peration, 'but you try getting the money to buy trucks to shift
it to hungry people.'

96

I have seen you in the circus
putting a merry-go-round together;

I have seen you in the petrol station
checking out a lorry's tyres;

and even patrolling roads
with your leather gloves and overalls.
. . .

You are God of the poor, a God human and simple;
A God who sweats in the street, a God of lined face.
And so I speak of you as my people speak;
You are a God Worker, a Christ Labourer.
. . .

Christ, O Christ Jesus, identify with us!
Lord, Lord my God, identify yourself with us!
Christ, Christ Jesus, be in solidarity with us!

> A Nicaraguan Peasant Mass boldly confesses its belief in a God who is involved in the joys and sorrows, the simple pleasures and hardships of Nicaraguan life.

97

Enable us, O Heavenly Father, to walk with thee this day and every day in sure and simple trust; ever remembering that our little things are all big to thy love, and our big things are small to thy power; through Jesus Christ our Lord.

98

Give me humility.
If Thou, Lord, had travelled in a sedan chair,
   how would the woman have touched thy garment's hem?

Henry Martyn, 1781–1812, reflecting on the incident recorded by Matthew, chapter 9

99

O Lord Jesus Christ, who travelled the roads of Palestine and made them serve the purposes of your kingdom, and who finally took the road to Calvary; extend your sharp eye, your consideration and your ready compassion to those of us who travel today's roads at such greater speeds, and who so sorely need the direction and protection you are able to give.

JBC

100

O Lord, I pray you
for all people who drive machines:
a locomotive, an airplane,

a car, a motorcycle, a scooter.
You know
that these people are often frivolous and tired.
And there have been terrible accidents
that drunks have caused.
How much misery and need
these dead
these injured,
these knocked-down people
have brought to their families!
Make these drivers more responsible.
Take them to task.
Your word is the only thing
that can change these fellows.
They are deaf and reckless
and show-offs.
You alone can make peace,
even peace on the roads.
Without it everyone
will want to go back to the bush.
And the other people
who use the roads
are school children,
women who are shopping or going to market,
men and other beings
that act like chickens on the road.
How often they are responsible for accidents!
Have these traffic victims prayed?
Have they forgotten
that you are our only Saviour and helper?
When they have not yet prayed,
or don't know how,
then we ask you,
heavenly Father,
to protect them from accident and danger.
Amen'

Ghanaian Christian

Dear St Christopher
Suffer not the drivers of the world
to put their trust in slogans and superstitions,
in fate and chance,
but to rely rather on your Lord's good gifts of patience
    and right judgement and helpfulness
for, like you, each one of us carries heavy responsibility
for the God-given lives of others.
May we feel the burden
but also know its privileges.

JBC

> How often one has travelled, fearfully, in erratically driven hill
> buses with '*Insha' allah*', or pictures of Hindu deities, over the
> driver's seat, or in badly driven cars bearing St Christopher
> badges!

102

Lord, I am a countryman
    coming from my country to yours.
Teach me the laws of your country
    its way of life
    its spirit
So that I may feel at home there.

      William of St Thierry, 1085–1148

Protecting prayers

103

Lord, help me not to dread what might happen
Nor to worry about what could happen
But to accept what does happen
Because you care for me.

104

O Lord, Jesus Christ, Son of God, deliver us from deception of the imminent, loathsome and cunning Antichrist and from all his evil designs.

Protect our spiritual father [*name of priest inserted*], all of us, his spiritual children and all our fellow Christians from his insidious traps, and shelter us within the hidden desert of Thy salvation.

Do not let us, O Lord, succumb to the fear of the devil, rather than abide in the fear of God, and let us not abandon Thee and Thy holy Church.

Better grant us, O Lord, to suffer and die for Thy holy name and the Orthodox Faith, rather than to renounce Thee; spare us from the Antichrist's seal of damnation and from worship of him.

Give us tears day and night, O Lord, to weep about our sins, and be merciful to us, O Lord, in the Day of Judgement.   Amen

Prayer of Russian Orthodox believers in the Soviet Union

105

Our Father, it is Thy universe, it is Thy will, let us be at peace, let the souls of Thy people be cool; Thou art our Father, remove all evil from our path.

African prayer

106

God, keep watch over our children so that we may again say 'good day' to them.

Prayer of Nandi fighting men, Kenya, off to war

107

Deliver us from the great imagined evils which may never come about.

108

As the banyan spreads her branches to give shelter to the traveller, so be thou a shelter to me; and when my journey is over, take me home to my native place – which is with you in Heaven.

Prayer from India

109

Keeper of the paths of men,
Hear a prayer for straightness.
Lord of the thin peaks,
Reared among the thunders,
Hear a prayer for courage.
Keeper of the headlands,
Holding up the harvest,
Keeper of the strong rocks,
Hear a prayer for staunchness.
Young Man, Chieftain,
Spirit of the Mountains!

Navajo Indian, New Mexico

Lord, if I have to die
Let me die;
But please, take away this fear.

Ken Walsh

Lord, help me not to waste a drop of my energy on fear and
anxiety, but grant me all the resilience I need to bear this
day.

Etty Hillesum, Dutch and Jewish, while awaiting deportation in
1941.

As we were walking along the Springfield Road towards
Spring Hill and Turf Lodge, four boys of seven or eight
years old caught up with us on their way home from school.
They were laughing and running. We all had to stop on the
kerb as an Army Landrover waited to cross the stream of
traffic on the Springfield Road.

The boys looked up smiling at the two soldiers, standing in
the back of the bullet-proofed Landrover, their automatic
weapons loaded at the ready.

'Hoo are y'?' shouted up one of the lads.
'Fine,' replied one of the soldiers, smiling back at the boys.
'How are you?'

'We're OK,' was the reply. '*Please don't shoot anyone today.*'

We walked on towards Spring Hill with that prayer in our
hearts.

John Martin, Corrymeela Community, Northern Ireland.

That prayer was surely echoed by the soldiers themselves, and
indeed by all of us on behalf of all troubled places in the world:
Please, God, let no one be shot anywhere today.

Lord, in these times when we are about to lose hope and our efforts seem futile, grant that we may perceive in our hearts and minds the image of your resurrection which remains our only source of courage and strength, so that we may continue to face the challenges, and struggle against hardship and oppression born of injustice.

Manila, Philippines. From a liturgy created for use by the people of one of the poorest slum areas.

114

O Lord God, who hast called Thy servants to ventures of which we cannot see the ending, by paths as yet untrodden, through perils unknown: Give us faith to go out with good courage, not knowing whither we go, but only that Thy hand is leading us, and Thy love supporting us; to the glory of Thy Name.

> Composed by Dean Eric Milner-White of York, and subsequently picked up by the Diocese of Blackburn in the United Kingdom, as originating in Bloemfontein, South Africa, and entitled 'Courageous Prayer', this is an interesting example of the way in which prayers, originally composed elsewhere, so exactly reflect and embody the needs of Christians in other parts of the world, that they even come to regard them as having been written by themselves and for themselves. This encourages us to use some of the great prayers of Christendom in other Church situations, knowing that if they are really great prayers they have universal currency and application.

115

We are a troubled frightened people, guns firing on our distant borders; we are afraid. Our fathers and forefathers fought for peace, but still peace eludes us.

Lord, we are tired, tired of the boasting of nations, tired of the tribal in-fighting, tired of the conflict of cultures, tired of our own unforgiving. We ask for your real peace which the world has failed to give.

Help us, Lord, to persevere in the seeking of your peace. Help us to know the only way to peace is the way of sacrifice. Help us to treat our fellow-men with dignity and respect because they bear your image. Then hasten, Lord, the time when we shall truly be united in one family with one living Lord, Jesus, Prince of Peace.

Janet Hopkins, wife of a priest working in the Transvaal, South Africa

116

O Thou, from whom to be turned is to fall,
    to whom to be turned is to rise,
    and in whom to stand is to abide for ever;
Grant us in all our duties Thy help,
    in all our perplexities Thy guidance,
    in all our dangers Thy protection,
    and in all our sorrows Thy peace;
    through Jesus Christ our Lord.

St Augustine of Hippo, 354–430

117

In thy journeys to and fro
    God direct thee;
In thy happiness and pleasure
    God bless thee;
In care, anxiety, or trouble
    God sustain thee;
In peril and in danger
    God protect thee.

Archbishop Timothy Olufosoye, Nigeria

God ever-present

118

And I will be with you all the time, to the very end of the world.

Matthew 28.20. 'The greatest of the promises ascribed to Jesus'

119

Dear God,
I just feel good knowing that you are
everywhere. That's all.

Swedish child

120

Where I wander – You!
Where I ponder – You!
Only You, You again, always You!
You! You! You!
When I am gladdened – You!
When I am saddened – You!
Only You, You again, always You!
You! You! You!
You above! You below!
In every trend, at every end,
Only You, You again, always You!
You! You! You!

Song of the Chasidic master, Levi Yitzchak of Berditchev, called
the Dudele

121

Called or not called, God is always there.

Carl Jung

122

If my servants ask thee about Me, lo, I am near.

From the Qur'an

123

'You have but to ask of Me,' says He,
'and I will give to you as I your need do see.

Be not filled with thought. Let me close the door
To all but Me, that in Me all things you adore.

My peace and joy upon you I bestow
If you but seek me in the place that's low.'

'Where is that place, dear Lord?' I begged in prayer.
'In the depth of your heart, my son, even in despair.

For if you find and feel Me in that place,
Then all the world becomes the time and space
in which you worship Me . . .'

Source unknown. Quoted in a Quiet Day in India

124

He prayed, but to his prayer no answer came,
and choked within him sank his ardour's flame;
No more he prayed, no more the knee he bent,
While round him darkened doubt and discontent;
Till in his room, one eve, there shone a light,
And he beheld an angel-presence bright,
Who said: 'O faint heart, why hast thou resigned
Praying, and no more callest God to mind?'
'I prayed,' he said, 'but no one heard my prayer,
Long disappointment has induced despair.'

'Fool,' said the angel, 'every prayer of thine,
Of God's immense compassion was a sign;
Each cry of thine, "O Lord!" itself contains
The answer, "Here am I"; thy very pains,
Ardour, and love and longing, every tear,
Are His attraction, prove Him very near.'
The cloud dispersed: once more the suppliant prayed
Nor ever failed to find the promised aid.

Jalaluddin Rumi, Persian mystic

125

I laugh when I hear that the fish in the water
is thirsty.
I laugh when I hear that men go on pilgrimage
to find God.

Kabir. Inscribed on the goldfish pond, Edwardes College,
Peshawar

126

This is the spirit that is in my heart, smaller than a grain of
rice, or a grain of barley, or a grain of mustard seed, or a
grain of canary-seed, or the kernel of a grain of canary-seed;
this is the spirit that is in my heart, greater than the earth,
greater than the sky, greater than heaven itself, greater than
all these worlds. This is the spirit that is in my heart.

Chandogya Upanishad

127

In every place where you find the imprint of man's feet,
there am I.

From the Talmud

To Him who is everywhere, men come not by travelling but by loving.

St Augustine of Hippo, 354–430

It does not behove thee, O man, to cross the seas, to penetrate the clouds, to cross the alps. No great journey is shown to you. If you wish to meet God, go as far as your own heart.

St Bernard of Clairvaux, 1090–1153

Thou art!
The hearing of the ear,
The seeing of the eye
Cannot reach Thee;
No 'How' or 'Why' or 'Where'
Can lead us to Thee.

Thou art!
Hidden is Thy secret,
Who may fathom it!
Deep, so deep,
Who can find it!

The Atta Nimsa: one of the Jewish prayers specially appointed for feast days.

One unforgettable day, dear God
You reached down to where I was
And lifted me up to where You are
And we have been inseparable
From that moment to this.

Ruth Harms Calkin: Prayer suggested for use by the Diocese of Lahore, United Church of Pakistan

The hope
we carry with us
is within

The faith
we offer life
is within

The love
with which we conquer life
is within

The truth
on which we found our life
is within

The road
we ever seek in life
is within

And what if
we should tear ourselves away
and step
deeper within?

Father Stanislaw Honoriusz Kowalczyk: 'Deeper and deeper within'

This Polish Dominican priest and Solidarity supporter, having fallen foul of the Polish authorities, died in a 'car accident' in May, 1983.

God's provision

133

I am happy because you have accepted me, dear Lord.
Sometimes I do not know what to do with all my happiness.
I swim in your grace like a whale in the ocean.
The saying goes: 'An ocean never dries up',
but we know that your grace also never fails,
Dear Lord, your grace is our happiness. Hallelujah!

Prayer from West Africa

134

O Heavenly Father, open wide the sluice gate into my heart
that I may receive thy living water and be fruitful.

Punjabi Christian

135

Writing of the second day of the memorable Kigezi Convention of 1945, destined to play such an important part in the East African revival, Dr Joe Church describes how African imagery began to enter into the exposition of Psalm 23, and in particular in relation to the words '. . . and my cup shall be full.' And so, he says, 'Another of the basic messages and prayers of the East African revival came to birth . . . We saw Christ Himself coming down and walking along the lines of seated people, with his golden pot filled with the water of life, waiting to fill to overflowing each cup, held out, and cleansed, the person's name written on each.'

And spontaneously, 'Pass me not, O gentle Saviour,' rose the words of the prayer/hymn from the massed throng, 'Do not pass me by!'

From J. E. Church, *Quest for the Highest*

Make me Thy cup and let my fullness be for Thee and for Thine.

Rabindranath Tagore

O Holy Spirit of God – come into my heart and fill me:
I open the windows of my soul to let Thee in.
I surrender my whole life to Thee:
come and possess me, fill me with light and truth.
I offer to Thee the one thing I really possess,
my capacity for being filled by Thee.
Of myself, I am an unprofitable servant, an empty vessel.
Fill me so that I may live the life of the Spirit:
the life of truth and goodness, the life of beauty and
    love,
the life of wisdom and strength.
And guide me today in all things: guide me to the people
I should meet or help: to the circumstances in which I
can best serve Thee, whether by my action, or by my
sufferings.

But, above all, make Christ to be formed in me, that I may
dethrone self in my heart and make Him king.
Bind and cement me to Christ by all Thy ways known and
unknown: by holy thoughts and unseen graces, and sacra-
mental ties; so that He is in me, and I in Him, today, and
for ever.

Meditative prayer to the Holy Spirit, by Walter Carey, Bishop of
Bloemfontein, 1921–34, and founder of the Village Evangelists.
He recommended that it be 'said slowly; or brooded over; or
thought and felt.'

My spirit is one with You, Great Spirit.
You strengthen me day and night to share my very best
    with my brothers and sisters.

You whom my people see in all of creation and in all people, show Your Love for us.

Help me to know, like the soaring eagle, the heights of knowledge.

From the Four Directions, fill me with the four virtues of Fortitude, Generosity, Respect and Wisdom; so that I will help my people walk in the path of understanding and peace.

Lakota prayer: St Joseph's Indian School, Chamberlain, South Dakota

139

Men and creatures are imparadised, O God, in thy love.
But who knows whence his blessings come to him!?
It is thou, O Lord, who art the true parent of all things.

Prayer of the Emperor Chia Ch'ing on the Altar of Heaven, Peking, China, the Winter Solstice, Dec. 21, 1539, proposed for Christian use.

140

Almighty God, source of love that endures forever, and source of all that is good; we praise and adore you.

God the weaver, we thank you for the rich tapestry of life, for the threads of love and laughter, and for the colour of emotion and imagination.

God the potter, we thank you for the gift of creation – for the shaping and moulding of individual lives.

God the carpenter, who took wood and shaped it into a symbol of hope for the whole of humankind, and . . .

God the host at every meal, who took everyday bread and wine and made it everlasting for the whole world.

Suggested for use by Christian Aid

God, I am in the wilderness – and find it very hard. It is hot during the day and cold during the night, and I am used to a moderate climate. The ground is sandy, and my feet are tired. I was excited when I started, but now . . .

God, I want to go back to Egypt. Not that I liked it there – it was hell and all that I was doing was making bricks. But at least I had learned to do it well, and there were many of us doing the same thing, day after day . . . But here I don't know anything. And what about food and water? In Egypt I wasn't getting much, but I knew I didn't have to worry about food . . .

God, I don't like to live in this tent – it has no foundations. Our homes in Egypt were not very good, but they had strong foundations. And here one wind will blow off the tent and it will be gone. What shall I do? . . .

God, How do I cross this ocean? And you are not performing any miracles either – You are just asking me to go forward. But how, Lord? . . .

God, I have some gold with me (I borrowed a lot of it when I left Egypt!) You know we like gold, and believe it can be useful. It gives us a sense of security. But what can I do with it in this wilderness? It is no use here! Shall I throw it away? But how can I? I had it with me all this time – and I may need it when I reach the Promised Land to buy milk and honey . . . I know what I will do; I will make a model in gold – oh yes, it is fun. Yes, it is beautiful; how I admire it. My gold and my craft . . .

God, I am nervous. I may not reach the Promised Land. You didn't say that *I* will get there. You only asked me to get out of Egypt. And I did . . . But where am I headed? I am eager to spell out my goals – but I don't find it easy, except that you have asked me to go forward . . .

God, help me to go forward, not because I know where I am going or how to get there . . . But *you* know. And you are with me – Emmanuel.

A seeker in India

God so loved the world

142

O God, let me feel this world as thy love taking form, then my love will help it.

Rabindranath Tagore

143

O God, I never listen to the cry of the animals or to the quivering of trees or to the murmuring of water or to the warbling of birds or to the rustling wind or to the crashing thunder without feeling them to be an evidence of Thy unity and a proof that there is nothing like unto Thee.

9th-century Sufi prayer

144

Blessed art thou, O Lord our God, King of the universe, Who hast such as these in thy world.

Jewish benediction: on seeing beautiful trees or animals

145

Lord of all creation, you speak to us through your creatures of your beauty and grace and humour and the loveliness of your form. So often, Lord, we take your gifts for granted, so often we are blind, so often we are brutal, so often we try to prove our superiority or make a profit out of your creatures. In their silence and suffering you rebuke us and sometimes by riding on a donkey you show us their beauty. Lord, this day let me not miss the loveliness of flowers or reject the loveliness of your animals, for if I do that, I fear I may miss you altogether.

Subir Biswas, Calcutta

146

Lord, forgive us for the joys we have not known.

147

May Africa praise you, you the true God
From the south even to the north,
From east to west, from sea to sea.
May the mighty wind bear your name
through cities and hamlets,
by quiet valleys and silent mountains,
over moving waters and sounding falls,
across the sunlit desert,
over the quivering savannah,
through the mysterious forest.
Across the immense African land, overflowing with your
    praise,
imprint all with your splendour which words cannot
    express.
May your name be known and loved all over the land.

Jerome Bala

148

*The congregation being summoned to the chapel by the call of
the conch shell, the following thanksgiving is offered:*

For the earth, and all that is part of it,
    we praise you,
For rocks (*appropriate available items being brought forward
and placed on the altar throughout the litany*), signs of your
strength and your steadfast love,
    we praise you,

WE PRAISE YOU FATHER (*and so after each sentence*)

For shells, signs of your variety and your joy in creating
    this world, which you have given to our care,
    we praise you.

For coconuts and taro, signs of your providence to us,
   we praise you.
For the birds, signs of the freedom that is ours when we
   recognise that we are your children,
   we praise you.
For the fish of the sea and animals that walk on the land, a
   reminder to us that the new earth is to be a place where
   your people live, work and share in peace,
   we praise you.
For insects, their variety, spontaneity and way of growth,
   signs of the dying and rising to new life that is the central
   message to us of your son Jesus,
   we praise you.
For the similarities of one group of people to another, signs
   of your desire that there be but one fold and one
   shepherd,
   we praise you.
For the differences between one group of people and
   another, expressed in this group through variety of language, tradition, custom, denomination, signs of the
   challenge of your word and your message to each person,
   we praise you.
For the people who are present at this celebration, who by
   their commitment, readiness to learn and to listen, and
   openness of heart and mind are signs of your readiness to
   forgive the wrongs we commit against you,
   we praise you.

Litany of praise from Melanesia

149

When I see the world from the moon on television, I want
to reach out and grab it for you, O Christ.

Billy Graham. Spoken in the opening address at the International
Congress on World Evangelisation, Lausanne

Your death, O Lord, we commemorate. Amen.
Your glory as our Risen Lord, now we celebrate. Amen.
Your return, as Lord in glory, together we await. Amen.

Mass on behalf of the Philippines

The practice of using the Creed, or some prayer, or act of faith
on behalf of a particular country is a common Catholic practice,
and might well be adopted by other traditions, and applied to
other lands.

151

Pour forth, O Christ, Thy love upon this land today.

152

Wide spaces, O Lord, and rural patterns, sundry peoples
and anxious days, as of old in Galilee when the Gospel first
was heard in the preaching of Jesus the Christ: Look now,
we pray thee, on thy Ugandan Church, that the Word may
be heard, disciples multiplied, evils exorcised and souls
healed. Give courage, patience and strength to all who go
forth in thy Name to serve and save their peoples, with
whom, as praying in that same Name, we are one even in
Jesus our Redeemer.

Bishop Kenneth Cragg

153

Grandfather,
Look at our brokenness.

We know that in all creation
Only the human family
Has strayed from the Sacred Way.

We know that we are the ones
Who are divided

And we are the ones
Who must come back together
To walk in the Sacred Way.

Grandfather,
Sacred One,
Teach us love, compassion, and honour
That we may heal the earth
And heal each other.

> Art Solomon: Ojibway Canadian

154

We remember, O Lord, our land and our nation before you.
In shame and humility we confess that we are a hopelessly
divided people, ruthlessly selfish, arrogant and conceited.
We are succumbing more and more to our carnal tendencies
giving vent to lewdness. We are prone to despise rather
than to love. Wrenching and hoarding appeal to us, and we
scoff at giving and sharing. We are suffocating goodness,
beauty and truth, and are rushing down the precipice of
ruin and destruction.

Lord, have mercy on us miserable offenders, forgive our
sins, renew and reclothe us with goodness, beauty, and
truth, and change us into instruments for the building of
your kingdom on earth. In Christ's name we pray.

> Prayer of confession from Calcutta

155

Lord God, lover of peace and concord, look down with
mercy upon Lebanon, that tormented country. Preserve its
people and guide its rulers. Bless the peacemakers and those
who love justice, defeat all men of evil will. May Lebanon
become again in your loving purpose a place of unity in
diversity, where men may learn to reverence life and
humankind as your creation.

This we ask through your Son Jesus Christ, our Lord and Redeemer.

156

Father in heaven, we give thanks for life, and the experience life brings us. We thank you for our joys, sorrows, trials, failures and triumphs. Above all we thank you for the hope we have in Christ that we shall find fulfilment in Him.

We praise you for our country, its beauty, the riches it has for us and the gifts it showers on us. We thank you for your peoples, the gift of languages we speak, the variety of races we have, the cultural heritage we cherish and the latent possibilities there are for our country to be great. Grant that we accept these gifts with thankfulness, and use them for the good of the human race and to bring glory to you. Through Jesus Christ our Lord. Amen.

Prayer of Thanksgiving for India

157

The children of Israel won their Promised Land
Built it
Nurtured it
Loved it.
Foreigners invaded
Destroyed
Enslaved
Exploited their religious culture
By demanding their songs
For selfish entertainment.
   The children of Israel were bold
   To lay their inner groanings
   Before their God –
   In honest words!
   This expression was founded
   On a solid faith
   In the strength of God . . .

A living reality
Throughout past history
Throughout the turbulent present
Throughout the unknown future.
We, the children of Zimbabwe
In order to move and prosper
As individuals
As a society
Offer our honest feelings
To our God.
We root our faith
In his continuing salvation
so that our feelings
Do not become a new prison
But a channel through which
Our soul may be restored.

Psalm of the children of Zimbabwe

158

Great Spirit of the islands and countries, Father of our Lord
Jesus Christ, we confess that we have seriously sinned in
words, deeds and thoughts. Forgive us, please, and gently
guide us in the ways of peace and love. Teach us to be more
caring and loving to our families and to others, and to be
more responsible in the task committed to us. Amen.

Prayer from Karibati, Micronesia

159

Lord, you want us to live in this city!
You know, Lord, this city is Hong Kong
a British Crown Colony on Chinese territory
founded on barren rock
established on business
filled with millions of refugees
supplemented with a minority of expatriates,
ante-chamber for missionaries hoping for the mainland,

governed by British subjects, ruled by money,
its factories producing consumer goods for export
its capital transferred to overseas banks
four and a half million people – we all live here –
yet who really feels at home in Hong Kong?
Lord, all people can feel at home in your presence.
May your people of Hong Kong extend the arms of your
love and compassion to all who live in this city.

Prayer for Hong Kong

160

I came to your shore as a stranger, I lived in your house as
a guest, I leave your door as a friend, my earth.

Rabindranath Tagore

161

By train this journey takes twenty-four hours.
It can be hot, dusty, noisy, crowded.
But this way it gives me less than one hundred minutes of
   air-conditioned ease in a soft seat, with refreshments
   served on the way.
Far below are circles of green on the brown plain –
Fields watered by patient irrigation.
Each patch with its cluster of houses in the centre.
And the villages are linked by long roads
Where the slow ox-carts travel.

The country is so great,
Too vast for any one man to know.
Yet each yard of road is known to someone or other,
Every green square the fruit of someone's toil,
Every least house has someone who calls it 'home'.
Only to you, Lord, is it all known perfectly.
No green patch, no foot of road, no toiling man is outside
   of your care, your knowledge or your love.

I kneel in spirit, and adore
A God great enough at once to see the whole
And to know intimately every smallest part.

Marjorie Prior, CMS mission partner: on flying from Delhi to
Bombay

162

God bless our home.

Carved in metal or on wood, this is a sentiment-cum-prayer widely
found in Jordan

163

Bless our home,
Father, that we cherish the bread
before there is none,
discover each other before we leave,
and enjoy each other for what we are,
while we have time.

Prayer from Hawaii

164

For your Fatherly love towards all mankind;
For sending your dear Son to redeem the whole world;
We thank you, good Father of us all.
For the obedience of his Mother to your special call;
For his humble birth in a carpenter's home;
We thank you, good Father of us all.
For his blessing the marriage at Cana;
For sharing in the home-life of Peter and Matthew;
For comforting Mary and Martha when bereaved;
For restoring Jairus' child to her family.
We thank you, good Father of us all.
For his welcome to children brought for his blessing;
For his concern for his mother, even from the cross;
We thank you, good Father of us all.

For breaking bread, as the living Lord, in the Emmaus
    house;
For using in his service Aquila and Priscilla and the
    witness and hospitality of innumerable families;
    We thank you, good Father of us all.
For sharing your Spirit with the whole household of
    faith, that it may become your new extended family
    with always room for more around the table.
    We thank you, good Father of us all.
Amen, so be it.

Litany of thanksgiving for homes, Andhra Pradesh, India

Prayers for people

165

O bless this people, Lord, who seek their own face under
the mask and can hardly recognize it . . .

O bless this people that breaks its bond . . .
And with them all, all the peoples of North and South, of
East and West,
who sweat blood and sufferings,
and see, in the midst of these millions of waves
the sea swell of the heads of my people,
and grant to them warm hands that they may clasp
the earth in a girdle of brotherly hands,
beneath the rainbow of thy peace.

Léopold Sédar Senghor: Prayer for peoples of other faiths and
ideologies

166

Grant us, O Lord, that we may never forget that every man
is the son of a King.

Hebrew Hasidim

167

Let me not shame the Father who displayest
thy glory in thy children.

Rabindranath Tagore

There is an old story about the rabbi who asked his disciples how they knew that night had ended and the day was on its way back. 'Could it be,' asked one, 'when you can see an animal in the distance and tell whether it is a sheep or a dog?' 'No,' the rabbi replied. 'Could it be,' asked a second, 'when you can look at a tree in the distance, and tell whether it is a fig or an olive tree?' 'No,' replied the rabbi. 'Well then, what is it?' the disciples pressed. 'It is when you look on the face of any man or woman, and see that he or she is your brother or sister. Because if you cannot do this, no matter what time it is, it is still night.'

O God, today and every day, help me to see all human beings as my brothers and sisters made in your image, and so may I always live in and by that light.

JBC

169

Grant us, O Lord, such a sense of our own value that we may convey to others a sense of theirs.

170

For every *woman* who is tired of acting weak when she knows she is strong, there is a *man* who is tired of appearing strong when he feels vulnerable.

For every *woman* who is tired of acting dumb, there is a *man* who is burdened with the constant expectation of 'knowing everything'.

For every *woman* who is tired of being called 'an emotional female', there is a *man* who is denied the right to weep and to be gentle.

For every *woman* who is called un-feminine when she competes, there is a *man* for whom competition is the only way to prove his masculinity.

For every *woman* who is tired of being a sex object, there is a *man* who must worry about his potency.

For every *woman* who feels 'tied down' by her children, there is a *man* who is denied the full pleasures of shared parenthood.

For every *woman* who is denied meaningful employment or equal pay, there is a *man* who must bear full financial responsibility for another human being.

For every *woman* who was not taught the intricacies of an automobile, there is a *man* who was not taught the satisfaction of cooking.

For every *woman* who takes a step towards her own liberation, there is a *man* who finds the way to freedom has been made a little easier.

Nancy R. Smith

Used in a mixed gathering, women and men saying sections appropriate to them, such a meditation has been found helpful in combating the stereotypes in which we so commonly place people.

171

The Jesus in me loves the Jesus in you

Affirmation suggested by Jean Coggan

172

Eternal God, as you created humankind in your image, women and men, male and female, renew us in your image:

God of the Holy Spirit, by your strength and love, comfort us as those whom a mother comforts:

Lord Jesus Christ, by your death and resurrection, give us the joy of those for whom pain and suffering become, in hope, the fruitful agony of travail:

God the Holy Trinity, grant that we may together enter into new life, your promised rest of achievement and fulfilment – world without end.

WCC Study Conference on The Community of Women and Men, Sheffield, England

173

Preeti is not unlike others –
   other dwellers in the slum.
She is imprisoned by indigence, illiteracy and ignorance;
She lives in her little hovel with her husband's three
   children;
Her mother and aunt frequent her place for food;
She is up against blank walls, several blank walls.
For Preeti, there hardly seems a way out,
Nobody to turn to, none to give a helping hand,
All her neighbours pity her, unpitying there is none;
But her state remains the same.

Yet Preeti has captured within her soul
Spontaneous, carefree, wholesome laughter,
Laughter that makes her forget her plight;
Her laughter is a sign of love.
Preeti laughs and Preeti loves,
She loves her husband's children,
Her neighbours she loves,
She loves the slum-dwellers, she loves the slum;
Preeti loves people, Preeti laughs;
It is sunshine to hear Preeti roar in laughter.
Her sparkling, overflowing, boisterous laughter
Free the neighbourhood from gloom to glee.

But Lord, the blank walls, several blank walls:
    Preeti has no means
    to feed her children thrice a day,
    to buy a cake on Christmas day,
    to have an outing once a year.

Make Preeti's laughter richer Lord,
By helping Preeti meet her needs.

M. A. Thomas, India

174

Our Father, how often have I said those words and yet you
have made them new for me in this hospital. How can I
thank you for the love, affection and concern of the stranger
which has upheld me through so many dark moments?
How can I doubt that the joyful chords of laughter that
have been built up in so short a time will find a place in
your kingdom in eternity? Help me always to be grateful as
you point to this man, this woman, and say, 'Son, behold
your mother and father, brother and sister.'

Subir Biswas, Calcutta

175

Lord Jesus, take away the veil from our eyes, that we may
contemplate the beauty of thy ideal. Grant to us thy power,
to the end that we may be faithful partakers of the joys and
sufferings of thy kingdom.

Tito de Alencar, Brazil

176

I thank Thee for Pain,
the sister of Joy.
I thank Thee for Sorrow,
the twin of Happiness.

Pain, Joy, Sorrow, Happiness.
Four angels at work on the Well of Love.

Pain and Sorrow dig it deep with aches.
Joy and Happiness fill it up with tears
that come with smiles.

For the seasons of emotion in my heart,
I thank Thee, O Lord.

Chandran Devanasen, India

177

We thank thee, God, for the equations of life – joy and pain, work and play, sun and rain, victory and defeat – that having one portion, we may understand the other also. Amen.

Prayer from Hawaii

178

God, who comes to us in our great joys, our crushing sorrows, and in our life day-to-day, be with us now as we share ourselves with one another in this time of . . . In Jesus' name we pray. Amen.

Open-ended prayer used to gather together the diverse range of human experience represented by delegates to the 6th WCC Assembly, Vancouver.

179

The blessing of the God of Sarah and of Abraham,
the blessing of the Son, born of Mary,
the blessing of the Holy Spirit who broods over us
as a mother over her children
be with you all. Amen.

Lois Wilson, Canada. Used at the 6th WCC Assembly, Vancouver

Prayers in helplessness

180

Almighty God. The hour of Thy glory has come; look mercifully upon me and deliver me from this great misfortune. In Thee I place my hopes. For alone I am helpless and as nothing. Help me, O God, and deliver me from fear.

From a Russian *samizdat* typewritten collection of prayers

181

Lord, the storm is done,
We could not keep it from coming;
we could not drive it away.
It came as a thief in the night.
Some were sleeping, Lord;
   Heal them
   Raise them from the dead.
Some were at work;
   Take away their fright
   Give them courage to pick up broken pieces.
The people are close to one another
   Foes are now friends
   Men have been tender
   Women have been brave
   Children have kept their faith
   Youth have matured in the storm.
It is a people, Lord,
and they are calling on your name.
Hear us as we huddle together, Christ,
Be in our midst
as storms come and leave us.

Tell the wild winds to be still, Christ,
Tell them to be still.

Prayer from the East Caribbean, after a hurricane

182

I do not know, O God,
What is there in store for me.
Only let me have your grace
To live with your blessing.

Prayer of Tamil awaiting repatriation to India

183

Like an ant on a stick both ends of which are burning, I go
to and fro without knowing what to do and in great despair.
Like the inescapable shadow which follows me, the dead
weight of sin haunts me. Graciously look upon me. Thy
love is my refuge.

Prayer from India

184

For what it's worth, here it is. Take it and use it. Use it for
the hungry, the homeless, the lonely; for the man down the
road who's lost both his job and his wife; for the friend
whose little girl has been killed. Use it to help me understand, to be less self-centred, more loving.

Mary Craig, in *Blessings*; to be said 'to whatever deity we pray
to'.

185

It is a strange experience to be working a regular seventeen-
hour day, and then suddenly to be immobilised and with-
drawn from the heart of a daily struggle in a city in the
pangs of rebirth. Yet this immobility is almost an urgent
prerequisite to rediscover the truth of the silence of God.

There is a hiddenness about God which can only be revealed to those who are not in an impossible rush to achieve targets. This is the strange paradox of God – God is in the midst of all struggle, in the midst of all change; in Him are consummated all our hopes and desires. Unless we discover Him in the struggle, we work in vain; and to discover Him, we have to stand still and know.

God, you have given to me so many gifts, so many eyes, so much desire, so little time to achieve what I see needs to be done and interpreted. Yet, Lord, sometimes you gently nudge me and remind me that I struggle in vain unless I can see you in the struggle, unless I stand still. Thank you for helping me to see that I have made work into a God, and lost my sense of direction and values. Thank you for stripping me of my physical power to do things, and for helping me with the feel of your hand in the dark – a hand whose texture I had forgotten. You do not grip very hard, Lord – sometimes you touch us so very gently – sometimes your advice is weak and your grip powerless. Help me, Lord, never to forget that in that powerlessness is you – help me never to cry in anguish when I lose my ability to achieve things – for perhaps then I am nearest to you – perhaps only then I can help your children most.

Subir Biswas: written in hospital in Calcutta.

186

Our experience is precisely that weakness is our strength, that the wind of the Spirit, within and outside the boundaries of the churches, has less to blow down when our structures are of mud and straw rather than concrete! Perhaps we should be thankful for our fragility; it is just that that keeps us on our toes.

Members of a Christian ashram, India

187

Lord Jesus, thou didst send us the missionaries and with them the Gospel, and for that we thank thee. Now thou dost wish to take the missionaries from us and our heart is alarmed. But thou dost deal justly with us. We have looked to the missionaries and not very much to thyself. Now thou takest them away so that we may look to thee alone and go forward with thee.

Prayer from New Guinea

188

O Lord, Thou givest the victory unto the weak! We give it to the strong and talented, but Thou givest it unto the weak. Amen.

Alexander Whyte, 1837–1921

189

Even, O God, if Thou givest me nothing I will thank Thee for everything.

One world

'No man is an island entire of itself' is the now very familiar
one-world image conveyed in John Donne's famous
seventeenth-century words, and developed by American
writer Nathan Scott, using equally memorable words.
'Nothing that exists is an island unto itself,' he declares.
'Everything that holds membership of the world is an
element of a seamless garment – the ragged edges of every
individual reality splay off into those of another, and the
world is a wedding.'

Beginning with the human husbandry of plants and animals, and our priesthood of the natural environment, the
prayers that follow then reflect our coinherence with the
world of saints and sages and good-folk-departed. They
then continue, less comfortably, to the subject of our unity
with fellow human beings, regardless of race and colour.
Here the injustices that exist between people; our propensity for war; the rivalries and divisions found among
Christians; the hardened attitudes that are sometimes
adopted in the relationships of men and women of different
faiths; all these and more tear that seamless garment almost
to the point of no-repair.

In the Christian view, however, repair is made possible
by love; such a love as is revealed in the life and death, and
continuing presence in the world, of Jesus Christ.

With this, then, as the overall pattern, the prayers that
follow do indeed splay off into each other; and hopefully
point to the celebratory conclusion that in Christ 'the world
is a wedding'.

190

Lord, there are lots of holes in my life.
There are some in the lives of my neighbours.

But if you wish, we shall hold hands.
We shall hold very tight,
And together we shall make a fine roll of fence to adorn
  Paradise.

Michel Quoist

191

The human race is to be seen as one great network of tissue
which quivers in every part when one part is shaken, like a
spider's web if touched.

Thomas Hardy. Quoted by Christian Aid as a thought on interde-
pendence.

192

All are each other's members, all mankind,
Since all of one sole ore have been refined.
One member's pain of body, heart or mind,
Means that the rest no lasting peace can find.
If you to share your brother's hurt declined,
Your claim to share the name of man you then resigned.

Sa'adi, Persian poet

193

Everyone of us is a part of the continent,
                 a part of the mainland;
Not one of us, an island.

We are men and women, one world household,
Participating together in the life of the mainland –
In our family,
    our neighbourhood
    our community
    our nation
    our community of nations.

We are none of us an island.

M. A. Thomas, India

May Divine blessing shower upon us.
May peace pervade the whole human race.
May there be an abundance of plants that we use.
May mankind prosper, O God, and animals flourish.
PEACE . . . PEACE . . . PEACE . . .

Hindu prayer

195

Hear our humble prayer, O God, for our friends the animals, especially for animals who are suffering; for any that are hunted or lost or deserted or frightened or hungry; for all that must be put to death. We entreat for them all Thy mercy and pity, and for those who deal with them we ask a heart of compassion and gentle hands and kindly words. Make us, ourselves, to be true friends of animals and so to share the blessings of the merciful.

Albert Schweitzer, missionary to Africa, 1875–1965

196

I would give nothing for that man's religion whose very dog and cat are not the better for it!

Rowland Hill, 1744–1833

197

We pray, Lord, for the humble beasts who with us bear the burden and heat of the day, giving their lives for the well-being of their countries; and for the wild creatures, whom you have made wise, strong and beautiful; we ask for them your great tenderness of heart, for you have promised to save both man and beast, and great is your loving kindness, O Saviour of the world.

Russian prayer

198

The milk-float,
the poor man begging,
the staircase and the lift,
the railway lines, the furrows of the sea,
the pedigree dog and the ownerless dog,
the pregnant woman,
the paper-boy,
the man who sweeps the streets,
the church, the school,
the office and the factory,
streets being widened,
hills being laid low,
the outward and the homeward road,
the key I used to open my front door;
whether sleeping or waking –
all, all, all
makes me think of You.

What can I give to the Lord
for all He has given to me?

Archbishop Dom Helder Camara, Brazil

199

Thou whose brow is of snow, whose eyes are of fire, whose
feet are more dazzling than gold poured from the furnace;
Thou whose hands hold captive the stars, Thou the first
and the last, the living, the dead and risen again; Thou
who dost gather up in Thy superabundant oneness every
delight, every taste, every energy, every phase of existence,
to Thee my being cries out with a longing as vast as the
universe, for Thou indeed art my Lord and my God.

Teilhard de Chardin

Prayer used at a Service of Thanksgiving for the life of Bishop
R. O. Hall of Hong Kong; a man, likewise, with a wide vision
of God's creation, and a passionate devotion to God's people
as part of it.

Lord,
Teach us that even as the wonder of the stars in heaven
only reveals itself in the silence of the night, so the wonder
of God reveals itself in the silence of the soul; that in the
silence of our hearts we may see the scattered leaves of all
the universe bound by love.

Adapted from the Bhagavad Gita, and used in the spiritual teach-
ing and devotions of Mother Teresa and her co-workers

201

In the immense cathedral which is the universe of God,
each man whether scholar or manual labourer, is called to
act as the priest of his whole life – to take all that is human
and to turn it into an offering and a hymn of glory.

Orthodox aspiration

202

The Communion of Saints in the Body of Christ is an exercise of the deep, sympathetic principle of humanity in the
power of regenerating grace. We hold communion one with
another, not as spirit with separate spirits, but as being one
Body, one Spirit, one Christ.

Attributed to Father R. M. Benson SSJE

203

Every history of ours, O Lord, is the history of all. For no
church is an island, entire to itself. For the fire of thy servants in far centuries, thy Name be praised, O Lord; for
ancient stones and liturgies, for ripened learning and long
disciplines of prayer and peace, thy Name be blessed, O
Lord, and every saint, O Lord, preserve, renew and
multiply, in the eternal Christ.

Bishop Kenneth Cragg

204

Let the glory of the saints, O Lord, illuminate the dullness of our hearts; that following the example of their lives on earth, we may shine with them in the everlasting light of heaven; through Jesus Christ our Lord. Amen.

205

Lord of the lovers of mankind who, for your sake, break the alabaster box of life, quicken your Church today with the ardour of the saints, so that by prayer and scholarship, by discipline and sacrifice, your Name may be made truly known.

Collect in commemoration of Ramon Lull of Tunis, in *A Calendar of Middle East Saints*, compiled by Bishop Kenneth Cragg

206

My brother, bridge the Christian centuries and touch us now;
    Least calm of all the saints,
    your white-hot African blood
    not stilled by your conversion to the faith.
Ranging among Algerian hills you tasted all
    our depths of self-despair
    before you reached in middle-life
    the calm of sin forgiven.
We need your strength in our slow decadence to understand
    re-birth through pain and hope
    and on this Gadarene hillside
    the sovereignty of God.

Randle Manwaring: Prayer in honour of St Augustine of Hippo

207

They call me African:
African indeed am I;
Rugged son of the soil of Africa,
Black as my father, and his before him;

As my mother and sisters and brothers,
living and gone from this world.

They ask me what I believe . . . my faith.
Some even think I have none
But live like the beasts of the field.
'Is it true,' they ask, 'that you believe
That the souls of your fathers hover around you,
In and out, wherever you go?'

Ah yes! It is true.
They are very present with us;
They speak to me in the wind and the rain,
Through fellow-man, and living creatures,
Birds of the air and reptiles gliding in the grass.
The dead are not dead, they are ever near us:
Approving or disapproving all our actions,
They chide us when we go wrong;
Bless us and sustain us for good deeds done,
For kindness shown, and strangers made to feel at home;
They increase our store, and punish our pride!

Why do you frown, dear friend?
Is this too much for you?
Is your Christian conscience scandalised?
Was it not one of your seers from the West who wrote:
'Dust thou art to dust returnest,
Was not spoken of the soul'?

Gabriel Setiloane, South Africa

This meditation is written in the characteristic style of African
Praise Songs which the South African recites before a chief on
important occasions. Here African Christianity brings its own
experience of holy communion with the departed to bear on
the Christian experience of the Communion of Saints. The
writer is one of the vice-presidents of the World Methodist
Council, and one-time Youth Secretary of the All African Conference of Churches.

O God of Abraham, Isaac, and Jacob, we beseech thee to hear the prayers of thy children whose ancestors knew thee not in this life. Thou knowest them all. Consecrate the bond of kinship which binds us to them, and mercifully make us partakers in him who died on the cross for the sins of the whole world, who preached to the spirits in prison, and rose again to be ruler over all thy creation, thy Son, our Saviour, Jesus Christ. To him, with thee and the Holy Spirit, be all praise and all glory, for ever and ever, world without end.

Daisuke Kitagawa, Japan

209

We give thanks to you, O Lord our God, for all your servants and witnesses of time past: for Abraham, the father of believers, and Sarah his wife; for Moses, the lawgiver, and Aaron, the priest; for Miriam and Joshua, Deborah and Gideon, and Samuel with Hannah his mother; for Isaiah and all the prophets; for Mary the mother of our Lord; for Peter and Paul and all the apostles; for Mary and Martha, and Mary Magdalene; for Stephen the first martyr, and for all the martyrs and saints in every age and in every land. In your mercy, O Lord our God, give us, as you gave them, the hope of salvation and the promise of eternal life; through Jesus Christ our Lord, the first-born of many fruits from the dead. Amen.

The Book of Common Prayer, Episcopal Church of the USA

210

Our Father, help us to know the light-year distance between one planet and another. Yet help us to know that the distance between one race and another can be even wider. Finally, lead us to know the ancient wisdom that love is the only bridge – between peoples, nations, and universes. Amen.

Prayer from Hawaii

. . . Divided all
In families we see our shadows born, and thence we know
That man subsists by brotherhood and universal love.
We fall on one another's necks, more closely and embrace
Not for ourselves, but for the Eternal family we live.
Man liveth not by self alone, but in his brother's face
Each shall behold the Eternal Father and love and joy
 abound.

> Quoted by China-watcher Joseph Needham in *The Dialogue
> between East and West*, with the comment: 'If we could only
> know the treasures of human experience of God contained in
> cultures which, because we will not work to understand them,
> seem so foreign to us, we should hug them to our breasts and
> cry out in amazement at the work of the Holy Spirit under all
> meridians.'

212

O Thou who art Father of all Mankind, who yet hast
sketched each one of us as an individual, help my family
to grow as a whole with members all covered with idiosyn-
crasies. Help me to respect the whole, and yet love the
odd details of a family. Amen.

Prayer from Hawaii

213

We in Africa never reject totally. We have such a strong
sense of the family of mankind.

Gabriel Setiloane, South Africa; answering questions

214

O Lord, our Lord, who hast decided that all men, whatever
their colour or race, are equal before thee: break down
the hatred between men, especially hatred due to national
differences. We ask thee to help those in whose hands are
the various governments of the world. Reconcile them to

one another, so that each may respect the rights of the other.

We ask all this in the name of our Saviour, Jesus Christ.

Student Christian Movement of Zambia

215

But you, Lord, have made us responsible for each other; for the neighbour, the stranger. This is the glory of your kingdom, you have put us in relationship, you have made us responsible with you. Help us, Lord, never to disown that responsibility. Help us never to forget that you are in all things and all things in you. This day if you put anyone in front of me help me to see you in them and to take responsibility.

Subir Biswas, Calcutta

216

Lord, you know that the buyers and sellers in our land are very special people. None of us can deceive you, neither the buyers, nor the sellers.
We know that this is not a laughing matter. Fraud is too often involved. Some people hunger, while others pile up riches. Let us as buyers and sellers keep our eyes on that. We want to pay what the goods are worth. But the others should not take more than they are worth. Bring peace there too, O Lord.   Amen.

Prayer from West Africa

217

Forgive us the wrong we have done,
as we have forgiven those who have wronged us.
When forgiveness is locked behind bared teeth
When resentment hides behind an affable mask
To forgive and to love are but inflated currency
on the stock exchange of deceitful good manners.
Wilt thou come to avenge or to forgive?

Wilt thou come to strike down in vengeance
or to lift up with a kiss?

Fridoline Ukur, Indonesia

218

Forgive us, Lord, when sometimes we think and act as if
only *we* have the devotion to you and to your children. We
need the strength of each other to continue to serve all your
creatures. Thank you for giving us companions on the way.

Subir Biswas of Calcutta, during his last illness, observing the
skill and devotion of so many people

219

O God, who has bound us together in this bundle of life,
give us grace to understand how our lives depend upon the
courage, the industry, the honesty and the integrity of our
fellow men, that we may be mindful of their needs, grateful
for their faithfulness, and faithful in our responsibilities to
them; through Jesus Christ our Lord.

Reinhold Niebuhr, 1892–1971

220

How is it possible for me to share the cup of the Lord's
blood with someone who I know denies me the chance to
share a cup of coffee?

Black South African delegate to the WCC Assembly, Nairobi

For those of us who pride ourselves on our freedom and ability
to share both the cup of the Lord's blood and a cup of coffee
or tea with those of any race, does not our membership of the
human family compel us to look at our reluctance to share the
good news of the Lord's shed blood with others, as well as our
failure to pay a fair price to the primary producers of that cup
of coffee or tea?

O Lord, help us to love people of all races, and so to act.

O Risen Christ, who made yourself known to the disciples
in the breaking of the bread at Emmaus; the bread we break
at this table is a sign of the brokenness of all the world;
through our sharing in the Bread of Life in our many Christian communions, open our eyes and hands to the needs of
all people. Let our hearts burn to share your gifts and help
us to go forth with one another with Bread: Bread of Hope,
Bread of Life, Bread of Peace.

Prayer used at the 6th WCC Assembly, Vancouver

222

Vouchsafe, we beseech thee, Almighty God, to grant to the
whole Christian people unity, peace and true concord, both
visible and invisible; through Jesus Christ our Lord.

A Book of Common Prayer, South Africa

223

Grant that in you, who are perfect Love, we may find the
way that leads to unity, in obedience to your love and to
your truth.

Thursday Candle, Community of the Resurrection, Mirfield,
England

224

O Christ, the peace of the things that are on high, and the
great rest of those that are below, establish O Lord in thy
peace and rest the four regions of the world, and principally
thy holy Catholic Church; and destroy wars and battles
from the ends of the earth, and disperse all those that
delight in war; and by thy divine mercy pacify the Church
and the Kingdom, that we may have a safe habitation in all
soberness and piety. And through thy mercy and love forgive the debts and sins of them that are departed this life.

Liturgy of Malabar, South India

225

God, what kind of world is this
that the adult people
are going to leave for us children?
There is fighting everywhere
and they tell us we live in a time of peace.
You are the only one who can help us.
Lord, give us a new world
in which we can be happy
in which we can have friends
and work together for a good future.
A world in which there will not be
any cruel people
who seek to destroy us and our world
in so many ways.   Amen.

Prayer written by a Liberian child

226

Help each one of us, gracious Father, to live in such magna-
nimity and restraint that the Head of the Church may never
have cause to say to any one of us, This is my body, broken
by you.

Prayer from China

227

O Lord, our fathers put spears into our hands and taught
us to use them. But you have put the book of life into our
hands; teach us to use it.

Prayer from Zaire

228

'There is no such thing as "Orange" tears and "Green"
tears [and we might add, "Catholic" or "Protestant" or
"Christian" or "Muslim" or "Hindu" tears]; we all weep
together'

Saidie Patterson, Shankhill, Northern Ireland

Grant unto all thy children, the believers, to live in the unity of the Spirit within thy fold, as one flock belonging to thee, O thou Chief Shepherd. Help us that we may all come to thee in one spirit, even though by various ways, all of them leading unto salvation through the blood of the Redeemer. Give us courage that we may kill all disputings and quarrellings among us believers, that we may be united, all of us, in thy love and thy obedience.   Amen.

Prayer of Egyptian Christians

230

O Lord, Jesus Christ,
Physician of souls
We beseech Thy healing touch upon
divided nations,
Church,
families,
neighbourhoods,
sick bodies,
troubled minds,
and broken hearts,
And bring us all, by thy grace,
to the gladness and glory of thy heavenly kingdom.

231

Lord, make us realise that our Christianity is like a rice field, that when it is newly planted, the paddies are prominent; but as the plants take root and grow taller, these dividing paddies gradually vanish, and soon there appears only one vast continuous field. So give us roots of love and make us grow in Christian fellowship and service, so that thy will be done in our lives, through our Saviour, thy Son, Jesus Christ.

Prayer from the Philippines

232

O God we thank you
for the wholeness of the human family:
for people of other faiths and of none, especially those
    who are our friends and neighbours;
for the rich variety of human experience and the gifts we
    bring to one another when we meet in a spirit of
    acceptance and love;
for dialogue in community, and for mutual enrichment
    and growing understanding;
for movements to establish and sustain the legitimate
    rights of persons of every religious conviction.
And we pray to you
that people of all faiths may enjoy the freedom to set forth
    their conviction with integrity and listen to one another
    in humility;
that the Church may perform a reconciling ministry in a
    world divided by suspicion and misunderstanding,
and bring healing to those places where religious
    intolerance fractures human community;
that the Church may bear a true and loving witness to the
    One it calls Lord, in whose name we pray.

                    Adapted for use at the 6th WCC Assembly, Vancouver

233

Our missions and evangelistic efforts
All seem like huge military campaigns –
As if we wage war,
A war against other believers
A crusade against men of other faiths,
Bent on annihilating unbelievers,
To fill the world with men of correct precepts.
We seem to have worked it out

The advance, The retreat, The supply line, The line of
defence, The plan for attack – A campaign to confound, to
conquer.

Today, Lord, you are calling us to drop the weapons of war.
You are summoning us to honest 'dialogue' in love,
Dialogue with other believers,
Dialogue with unbelievers,
Dialogue with men of other faiths;
For your Son Jesus Christ died for them too,
The victory won over death is theirs too.

What is this 'dialogue'?
Is it perhaps a new method of warfare?
Is it, maybe, a subtle way to proclaim the Christian news?
Is it a strategy of convenience?

Is there something more in dialogue – more substance?
Tell us, Lord, what this substance is.

                                           M. A. Thomas, India

234

'What is the use of argument and controversy?' the gentle, saintly Maulvi Zaka Ullah of Delhi would say. 'Tell me your Beautiful Names for God, and I will tell you mine.'

                C. F. Andrews in *Memoir: Zaka Ullah of Delhi*

235

Eternal God, whose image lies in the hearts of all people, we live among peoples whose ways are different from ours, whose faiths are foreign to us, whose tongues are unintelligible to us.
Help us to remember that you love all people with your great love, that all religion is an attempt to respond to you, that the yearnings of other hearts are much like our own and are known to you.
Help us to recognise you in the words of truth, the things of beauty, the actions of love about us.

We pray through Christ, who is a stranger to no one land more than to another, and to every land no less than to another.

Used at the 6th WCC Assembly, Vancouver

236

O Lord, thou has decreed that all shall belong to the same household.

Baha'i prayer

237

O God, the Parent of our Lord Jesus Christ, and our Parent: thou who art to us both Father and Mother: We who are thy children draw around thy lotus feet to worship thee. Thy compassion is as the fragrance of the lotus. Though thou art enthroned in the heavens, we may draw nigh to thee: for thy feet stand upon the earth where we humans dwell. Thy Son, our Lord, was man.

We see thy compassion in Jesus. He gives content to the Hindu name for thee – Siva, the Kindly One. He gives significance to the Muslim address of thee – Allah, the Merciful. He embodies in the Godhead what the Buddhist worships in the Buddha – compassion itself.

Thou God of all the world, let our history teach us that we belong to thee alone and that thou alone dost belong to us. And thou art enough, for in thee we sinners find sonship and daughterhood again – the one thing that we most need.

D. T. Niles, Sri Lanka

238

Father of all Mankind, make the roof of my house wide enough for all opinions, oil the door of my house so it opens easily to friend and stranger, and set such a table in my house that my whole family may speak kindly and freely around it.   Amen.

Prayer from Hawaii

Lord, as you have entered into our life and death and in all the world you call us into your death and risen life, draw us now, we pray, by the power of your Spirit, into an exchange of gifts and needs, joys and sorrows, strength and weakness with your people everywhere; that with them we may have grace to break beyond every barrier, to make disciples of all nations and to share the good news of your love with all mankind for your glory's sake.

CMS Interchange prayer

240

Lord, today you made us known to friends we did not
  know,
And you have given us seats in homes which are not our
  own.
You have brought the distant near,
And made a brother of a stranger,
Forgive us, Lord . . .
We did not introduce you.

Prayer from Polynesia

241

Heavenly Father, we give thanks for the living, loving Spirit, releasing us from old fears and prompting us to new ventures. Fit us by thy grace to realise more ardently the fellowship which is ours in Christ, and to extend it generously across all frontiers, through Jesus our Lord.

Collect in commemoration of Cornelius-of-the-Palestinian-Shore, in *A Calendar of Middle East Saints*, compiled by Bishop Kenneth Cragg

242

Blessed art thou, O Christ our God, who didst reveal thy wisdom to simple fishermen, sending upon them from above thy Holy Spirit, and thereby catching the universe as in a net. Glory to thee, O thou who lovest mankind.

Troparion for Pentecost: from a Russian Orthodox Liturgy

243

O God, we thank thee that in faith we are Children of Abraham and share in the promise of universal blessing. Open our eyes and hearts to his other children, Jews and Muslims, and inspire us to work with them to bring their promised blessing to all generations. We offer this prayer in the memory of the love shown on the cross, and in the faith that in Jesus thou thyself hast provided a lamb to take away the sins of the world.

Peter Schneider: Suggested alternative Collect for Good Friday

244

Source of truth and Lord of all life, it was your Son Jesus Christ who taught us to call you 'Father' and to acknowledge that none may come to you except through him; enable us to recognise with gratitude those elements of truth and justice in other beliefs; encourage us to love and care for those who search for you under other names, but keep us from ever denying the uniqueness of Jesus, and fire us with the desire to make him known as mankind's only Saviour and Lord. In the name of Jesus.

Michael Saward: *Task Unfinished*

245

O God who hast made of one blood all nations of men for to dwell on the face of the earth, and didst send thy blessed Son Jesus Christ to preach peace to them that are afar off, and to them that are nigh; Grant that all the peoples of the world may feel after thee and find thee; and hasten, O Lord, the fulfilment of thy promise to pour out thy Spirit upon all flesh; through Jesus Christ our Lord.

Bishop Cotton, 1813–66. Prayer for India

246

O God, who created all humankind in your own likeness
we thank you for the wonderful diversity of races and
   cultures in this world.
Enrich our lives by ever widening circles of fellow-feeling
   and understanding;
show us your presence in those most different from us,
so that both by what we have in common,
and in those things in which we differ, .
we may come to know you more fully in your creation.

JBC

247

O thou who didst create light pure and clear,
yet refracted into the many colours of the rainbow:
Grant that we who see thee
each from our own vision,
may in sharing our experience with one another
see thee more nearly as thou art
in all thy truth and beauty.
Let each Church bring its heritage
of truth and worship
that the full inheritance may be revealed
and made available for all who call thee Father,
through him in whom the fulness of thy glory dwells,
even thy Eternal Son, Jesus Christ our Lord.

George Appleton

Under lock and key

248

As we closed our doors this morning, and walked freely through the church door, other doors slammed behind other people, and they do not know if or when they will be open again; doors in prison cells and torture chambers; doors separating families; doors in labour camp units. Let us ask Christ, who came to set all men free, to enable us to experience his freedom and to bring that freedom to others.

Prayer for prisoners of conscience: Pax Christi

249

O Lord, I sing thy praise
In the turmoil and darkness
Of the heathen temple.
Thou art, O Lord, indescribable, incomparable,
Invisible and omnipresent . . .

And here am I who speak of meaning,
The meaning of my life in this world.
Mine is the right to decide,
Choice and action,
Thou art word and meaning, thou the observer.

I love thy grass, O Lord,
The sun, and murmurs in the night,
The woman whom I have yet to meet,
The book I have yet to write.

I love the fragrance,
        the sounds,
        the colours
Of flowers, of the sea, of birds. Of freedom.

But still more I love meaning:
That the tree may grow from the earth,
Man from boy
And word from Truth.
The meaning of the sweet grace
The salt sea,
The bitter cloud,
But not of the sweet lie
And bitter freedom.

I have learned to see sweetness
In barbed wire thorns,
In Ural snows,
In smiling prison guards
I have understood that even
Four months' fast may be sweet,
Without grapes, without the sea.
In the smells,
        sounds,
        sights
Of the concentration camp
I have felt and understood
The sweetness of Freedom.

My word grew from my truth,
My truth from my meaning,
But word, truth, meaning and I myself
From the world, O Lord.
Mine is the right to decide
And I have chosen.
In the cold, amidst violence,
I have chosen, O Lord,
The meaning of Freedom.

                    Psalm: Semyon Gluzman.

A Soviet Jewish psychiatrist known to have denounced the
political abuse of psychiatry in his country, he was subsequently, in 1972, exiled first to a concentration camp and
then to a regional agricultural centre in the Ural Mountains,
from where he wrote this psalm.

O Lord Jehovah,
Here in this unlikely place
we remember your children of long ago, who
in the brickfields of Egypt
suffered so sorely at the hands of Pharaoh,
So that by reason of their great bondage
they could not hear your voice.
Have pity on all such in the world today
whose lot is so similar to theirs:

those in forced labour camps in the Soviet Union and East-
ern Europe; Palestinians on the West Bank; those restricted
to living in the black townships of Southern Africa; those –
specially the young ones – working in the sweatshops of
South-east Asia; all who suffer any kind of oppression of
mind or body.

So, as we recall that the first Passover occurred in such
inauspicious circumstances – that Moses's meeting with
you and your promise of deliverance happened in a brickyard – we ask that by your outstretched arm you will deliver
all such, even today.

And as for us, with our secure houses and brick-built churches, may all brickyards remind us of the costly tradition
of social justice and concern on which our faith is built.

JBC: On seeing a brickyard, anywhere (Exodus 5).

For those who grasp their prison bars helplessly, that we
may walk free –
    a thought.

For those who rot in the dark so that we may walk in the
sun –
    a thought.

For those whose ribs have been broken so that we may
   breathe our fill –
      a thought.

For those whose back has been broken so that we may walk
   erect –
      a thought.

For those whose faces have been slapped so that we may
   walk in fear of no hand –
      a thought.

For those whose mouths have been gagged so that we may
   speak out –
      a thought.

For those whose pride lies in rags on the slabs of their jails
   so that we may proudly walk –
      a thought.

For those whose wives live in anguish so that our wives may
   live happy –
      a thought.

For those whose country is in chains so that our country
   may be free –
      a thought.

And for their jailers and for their torturers –
      a thought.

The saddest of all, they are the most maimed, and the day
   of reckoning is bound to come.

                    Salvador de Madariaga: Amnesty International

252

Forgive them all the tortures done,
   My thirst and my starvation;
For who would suffer more than One
   Who died for our salvation.

One of the stanzas of a three-verse poem written on the wall of his cell by an English prisoner of war, before his execution at the hands of the Japanese, in which he unites himself to the suffering Redeemer, and prays for his murderers.

253

Peace to all men of evil will. Let vengeance cease and punishment and retribution. The crimes have gone beyond measure, our minds can no longer take them in. There are too many martyrs . . . Lord, do not weigh their sufferings on your scales of justice, and let them not be written in their act of accusation and demand redress. Pay them otherwise. Credit the torturers, the informers and traitors with their courage and strength of spirit, their dignity and endurance, their smile, their love, their broken hearts which did not give in even in the face of death, even in times of greatest weakness . . . Take all this into account, Lord, for the remission of the sins of their enemies, as the price of the triumph of justice. Take good and not evil into account. And let us remain in our enemies' thoughts not as their victims, not as a nightmare, but as those who helped them to overcome their crimes. This is all we ask for them.

Prayer for forgiveness, offered by one who died in a concentration camp

> In not a few cities in Pakistan, down some little side street, outside a newspaper office, near a university, or in a *chowk* or square reserved for public meetings, the passer-by will suddenly come upon some little impromptu memorial shrine – immediately cleaned up when spotted by the authorities – a heap of flowers, a twist of tinsel, a number of photographs, and – by night – sometimes a group of guttering candles or a small oil lamp showing up a message hastily splashed onto a wall – 'Here . . . students were killed.'

O Lord, Jesus Christ, whose perfect love met death by violence and was not extinguished; so enter the hearts and minds of those affected by violence, that frailty may give way to your strength, loss to your gain, bitterness to your total and victorious love; for your name's sake. Amen

Susan Williams

254

Lord, we call to mind all authority that treats people as nobodies –

Military regimes and dictatorships,
lonely prisons and unjust laws,
the war industry and political greed.

Used at the 6th WCC Assembly, Vancouver

255

Grant peace and eternal rest to all the departed, but especially to the millions known and unknown who died as prisoners in many lands, victims of the hatred and cruelty of man. May the example of their suffering and courage draw us closer to Thee through Thine own agony and passion, and thus strengthen us in our desire to serve Thee in the sick, the unwanted and the dying wherever we may find them. Give us the grace to spend ourselves for those who are still alive, that we may prove most truly that we have not forgotten those who died.

Sue Ryder and Leonard Cheshire

This prayer hangs in the Sue Ryder Home, Cavendish, Suffolk, England.

256

Speaking of signs
before or after miracles
speaking of signs
at all . . .
I have often wondered
about those

who had broken
the bread
and had drunk
the wine
for the very first time:

By the same token . . .
what paths did their thoughts follow
while waiting for the completion of the rite
transforming bread into flesh
and wine into blood . . .
With what doubts about future persecution
with what fears about solitary confinement
did they partake with trembling lips
of these blessed morsels
of You
dear Lord?

By the same token . . .
kneeling,
praying . . .
hearing
the murmured words
of the priest
I too am cleansed
in remembrance of You;

am filled with wonder anew –
despite our awesome technologies,
our probing gods of psychoanalysis,
our high priests of political ideology
– that You, Lord,
have remained the same solid assurance
now! as you were then . . .
By the same token,
Lord!
By the same token!

Van van Rensburg, South Africa

In Namibia, with many South Africans and Namibians fighting each other, four young men, in obedience to their Christian conscience, refused to do military service and were sent to jail. This appeared in *The Sword*, St Alban's Cathedral, Pretoria, and is dedicated to one such young man, Charles Yeats, Diocesan Secretary of Namibia.

257

Thank you, Lord Jesus,
that you will be our hiding place
whatever happens.

Corrie ten Boom

A prayer recollecting the secret room in her Amsterdam home in which her father sheltered Jews, and which led to the family's imprisonment in Ravensbruck.

258

'What saved me was prayer and fasting,' declared a newly released prisoner of conscience. While in a death-camp he received a piece of bread every two or three days, and made this 'imposed fast' an 'offered fast', which strengthened him physically and spiritually. The continuous repeated praying of the 'Our Father' was his nourishment, and prepared him for all events.

Our Father in heaven,
hallowed be your Name,
your kingdom come,
your will be done,
on earth as in heaven.
Give us today our daily bread.
Forgive us our sins
as we forgive those who sin against us.
Do not bring us to the time of trial
but deliver us from evil.
For the kingdom, the power, and the glory are yours
now and forever. Amen.

Service of Holy Communion, Series 3

Square my trial to my proportioned strength.

John Milton, 1608–74

Teach me, O Lord, to accept these manacles as my wedding ring to Christ.

> Prayer of a 'Gallerien', a man condemned to the horrors of the galleys; in this case a French Protestant of the 17th-century, savagely persecuted for his faith.

261

O Lord, whose holy saints and martyrs in all times and places have endured affliction, suffering and tribulation, by the power of the Holy Cross, the armour of salvation: so likewise, we pray, send your Holy Spirit, the Comforter and Advocate of all Christians, to sustain these churches in their martyrdom, witness and mission. The world without provocation hates your Church, but you have taught us not to despair. Therefore, you who are a God at hand and not a God afar off, grant to these Christians the power to lift up their hands, their eyes and their hearts to continue their living witness in unity with the universal Church, to the glory of your most holy name.

Romanian Christian

262

Who can boast of being free?

Who has not got
secret prisons,
invisible chains,
all the more constricting
the less they are apparent?

Archbishop Dom Helder Camara, Brazil

263

Peter-in prison
for whom the church offered prayer without ceasing
and who was wonderfully released:
come to our aid.

Paul-in-prison
whose every experience of captivity was turned to good
    purpose
and who held himself never to be a prisoner of men or of
    circumstances
but always 'the prisoner of the Lord':
come to our aid.

Blessed Jesus-in-prison
unto death, and resurrection . . .
who visited imprisoned spirits and preached liberty to the
    captive
and out of overwhelming goodness burst open every
    prison:
come to our aid.

JBC

264

Remember, my God, the fall of Lucifer full of pride; keep
me safe with the power of your grace; save me from falling
away from you, save me from doubt. Incline my heart to
hear your mysterious voice every moment of my life. Incline
my heart to call upon you, present in everything.

Glory to you for every happening, every condition your
providence has put me in.

Glory to you for what you speak to me in my heart.

Glory to you for what you reveal to me, asleep or awake.

Glory to you for scattering our vain imaginations.

Glory to you for raising us from the slough of our passions through suffering.

Glory to you for curing our pride of heart by humiliation.

Glory to you, O God, from age to age.

Fr Gregory Petrov, Russian Orthodox protopriest

Fr Petrov composed the akathist 'Glory to God for All Things' – from which the above prayer is taken – just before he died in prison in the early 1940s. The title is from the words from St John Chrysostom as he was himself dying in exile. It is a song of praise from amidst severe suffering.

Prayers of compassion

265

O perfect master, You shine on all things and all men, as gleaming moonlight plays upon a thousand waters at once! Your great compassion does not pass by a single creature. Steadily and quietly the great ship of compassion sails over the sea of sorrow. You are the great physician of a sick and impure world.

From the Buddhist spiritual treatise, *Amidista*

266

Lord, the stars float from Thy hands
like silver bubbles.
The clouds wrap themselves round Thy fingers.
Rivers flow across Thy palms which are covered
with miles of forest and green fields and lakes
that have formed in their hollows.
Suns flash from Thy forehead.
Universes dance about Thy feet . . .

And yet, O Lord,
Thou didst tread the dusty road
that led to Golgotha.
Thou didst hang upon a cruel cross
for love of mere men.

Chandran Devanesen, India

267

Christ,
I have climbed up to you from the filthy, confined quarters down there, with their stench of urine and typhoid fever . . . to put before you, most respectfully, these considerations:

There are nine hundred thousand of us down there in the slums of that splendid city, and the number keeps increasing . . .

And you, Christ,
Do you permit things like that? Why? Did you not come to help the world?

Christ,
Do not remain here at Corcovado surrounded by divine glory. But go down there into the *favelas*. Come with me into the *favelas* and live with us down there. Don't stay away from us; live among us, and give us new faith in you and in the Father. Amen.

Prayer from Rio de Janeiro, Brazil

> Using such words, a poor man climbs up from the *favelas* of Rio de Janeiro, and addresses the colossal Christ of Corcovado; and adds the comment, 'If Christ did go into the *favelas* in the person of Christians and their priests, the poor man would not become a communist. Christians and communists could even meet in the poor man's house and, though his friendship, could become friends together, and Christ would be among them.'

268

This is a long wait at the bus stop:
It is quite late – we must get home.

Here it comes,
It didn't stop – it just went by;
It seemed all filled up.
It just went past without stopping;
We are still waiting to get on.

We're thinking,
Oftentimes we pass by others,

Others who are waiting, eagerly waiting,
  Waiting to get on,
  Waiting to have a word,

Waiting to be heard,
Waiting for a friendly gesture,
Waiting for a smile, a kind look
  – we've passed by.

Why, Lord, why do we pass by?
Like the bus we are filled up, too;
We are filled up with ourselves,
    our worries – our joys,
    our hates – our loves,
    our fears – our hopes,
    our failures – our victories,
    our wants – our riches,

We are filled up with ourselves.

We are filled up,
And we pass by.

                    M. A. Thomas, India

269

When I gave nothing
but money
I gave nothing
of me.

God,
but when you bade me
to give as well
of my intellect
time and reasoning;
the faceless mob
consuming my gifts
broke apart into individuals
each donning his own peculiar
    personality,
each offering himself
    as a gift
to me.

Thank you God for this
your greater gift
in return for
your gift – compassion!

Meditation from Pretoria, South Africa: intellect, time and reasoning as constituent parts of compassion.

270

Poverty is
- a knee-level view from your bit of pavement;
- a battered, upturned cooking pot and countable ribs;
- coughing from your steel-banded lungs, alone, with your face to the wall;
- shrunken breasts and a three-year-old who cannot stand;
- the ringed fingers, the eyes averted, and a five-paise piece in your palm;
- smoking the babus' cigarette butts to quieten the fiend in your belly;
- a husband without a job, without a square meal a day, without energy, without hope;
- being at the mercy of everyone further up the ladder because you are a threat to their self-respect;
- a hut of tins and rags and plastic bags, in a warren of huts you cannot stand up in, where your neighbours live at one arm's length across the lane;
- a man who cries out in silence;
- nobody listening, for everyone's talking;
- the prayer withheld;
- the heart withheld;
- the hand withheld; yours and mine.

Lord, teach us to hate our poverty of spirit.

Litany from Calcutta

Christians have lessons to be learnt from cemeteries, gutters and dustbins, and not only from the lives of Saints!

Ivor Smith-Cameron

272

Am I mistaken, Lord,
is it a temptation to think
You increasingly urge me
to go forth and proclaim
the need and urgency
of passing
from the Blessed Sacrament
to your other presence,
just as real,
in the Eucharist of the poor?
Theologians will argue,
a thousand distinctions be advanced . . .
But woe to him who feeds on You
and later has no eyes to see You,
to discern You
foraging for food among the garbage,
being evicted every other minute,
living in sub-human conditions
under the sign
of utter insecurity!

Archbishop Dom Helder Camara, Brazil

273

Lord, forgive us the contents of our dustbins, and help us to recognise you in every refuse collector.

JBC

O blessed Jesus! Do you remember the day we went out with a choir from Puerto Rico and they were ill in Cerro Gordo? About thirteen youngsters were taking turns to use the toilet that morning, boys as well as girls. I'm reminding you, Jesus, because in experiences like these we have come a bit closer to the reality of the people we are trying to save. In our new Columbia, Jesus, 200,000 people live on miserable settlements, with no drinking water. Six thousand families live piled together in the Majaguas terraces. There is one toilet for every four families. Dona Flor found out that their biggest problem is having to look after the girls when they go to the toilet, because if they go alone the caretakers take advantage of it and assault them.

Visiting a lavatory is not an act of 'good taste'. Writing about the experience is worse – and mentioning it to readers can cause offence. But a large part of this ministry can be found there, Jesus. We live in the filth, we breathe it until our lungs are saturated. To be poor means to live in squalor. As you will see, we have learned to read the Bible with these people from their point of view. I am convinced that if you take notice of them it is because they no longer have anyone on whom they can depend or to whom they can go for help. It is by breathing in the Spirit that their conscience is made clean. You are the one who keeps their rebellious instinct in check. Mind you, Jesus, they do suffer and they only rebel when they can't take any more. The poor are a generous and noble people. That is why, when they asked me to dedicate a lavatory, I went and dedicated it with all solemnity. That lavatory is a guarantee that from now on fewer children will die of worms in that neighbourhood. You, who loved the children so much, inspire me to do this work. And so we press on and we'll meet on the way, Lord.

Juan Marcos Rivera: A Letter to Jesus

Lord, I am ashamed. I have so much and others so little. I am ashamed to be part of the society which has no value for such a man. Lord he is your child, made in your image and you have an eternal purpose for him. Help me to learn from him. All day, every day, he does the same work, lowly perhaps degrading, but a great benefit. He works honestly and without pretence. Lord, I am stupid, help me to see that you value him and many others like him whom we take for granted and so seldom give recognition or extend a human hand of friendship. Lord, I thank you for him. Help me to become a little like him, for I realise that to men like him, poor in spirit, is given your kingdom.

Subir Biswas of Calcutta, of the man who gave him his bedpan each day and cleaned him up, during his last illness

276

While you are Jesus,
my Patient,
deign also to be to me a patient Jesus,
bearing with my faults,
looking only to my intention
which is to love and serve you
in the person of each of your sick.

Prayer offered daily by Mother Teresa's helpers in Shishu Bhavan, Calcutta

277

Lord, I am two men
And one will labour to the end
And one is weary already
Have compassion on me.

Lord, I am two men
And one knows the suffering of the world
And one knows only his own
Have compassion on me.

278

Lord, let me share

279

If only I may grow firmer, simpler, quieter, warmer.

Dag Hammarskjold: *Markings*

280

My Lord and God, take all from me that blocks my way to
Thee.
My Lord and God, give all to me that speeds my way to
Thee.
My Lord and God, take this self from me and give it as
thine own to Thee.

Nikolaus von der Flue, the Swiss mountain saint

In his autobiographical journal, *Part of a Journey*, Philip
Toynbee asks himself whether he would be willing to take a
Vietnamese boat family into his home, and, with characteristic
honesty, regretfully concludes that he would not, using this
prayer.

281

Nothing seems to be moving,
It is still – so very still,
We cannot feel the world around us;
We do not hear the people around us,
We do not care,
We do not listen,
We want to be by ourselves.

Lord:

We want to look at the stars in the sky,
We want to see the sun rise in the east,
We want to hear the clangour of the thunder,

We want to feel the wind blowing in our faces,
We want to feel the rain falling on our outstretched hands,
We want to feel the sun scorching our backs.

We want to hear the grief of Mary next door
We want to see the happiness of Nalini and Satish,
We want to know the frustrations of young Srini,
the successes of sportsman Hari,
the hopes of the journalist Setta,
the fears . . . of people surrounding us.

Lord:

Lead us from indifference to solicitude;
Lead us from insensitivity to sympathy;
Lead us from inertia to alertness.

Lord we want to care, we want to hear.

M. A. Thomas, India

282

Almighty God, full of mercy, look down with pity upon all
the innkeepers of the world who turn guests away because
of their colour or creed or condition. Prepare room in our
hearts that those who are hurt or rejected or ignored in the
world may find kindness there. In the Name of One who
had to be born in a stable. Amen.

Prayer from Hawaii

283

Make us worthy, Lord, to serve our fellow human beings
throughout the world who live and die in poverty and
hunger.

Through our hands, grant them this day their daily bread;
and by our understanding love, give them peace and joy.
Amen.

Co-Workers of Mother Teresa, daily prayer

O Merciful and loving Father of all, look down we pray
thee on the hungry millions in the world today who are at
the mercy of disease. Grant that we who live so comfortably
and gently may have true sympathy with them and do all
in our power to help them to that abundant life which is
thy will; through Jesus Christ our Lord. Amen.

George Appleton

285

God's right hand is gentle, but terrible is his left hand.

Rabindranath Tagore

286

The right hand of God is *striking* in our land
Striking out at envy, hate and greed.
Our selfishness and lust, our pride and deeds unjust
Are destroyed by the right hand of God.
The right hand of God is *healing* in our land,
Healing broken bodies, minds and souls.
So wondrous is its touch,
With love that means so much,
When we're healed by the right hand of God.
The right hand of God is *planting* in our land,
Planting seeds of freedom, hope and love.
In these Caribbean lands
Let his people all join hands
And be one with the right hand of God.

Patrick Prescod, the Caribbean: from the song 'The Right Hand
of God'

287

Grant, O God, your protection; and in your protection,
strength; and in strength, understanding; and in under-

standing, knowledge; and in knowledge, the knowledge of justice; and in the knowledge of justice, the love of it; and in that love, the love of existence; and in the love of all existence, the love of God, God and all goodness.

Ancient Welsh prayer

Prayers for creaturely needs

288

Lord, receive our praise and adoration.
O Creator of the world, stay with us always.

You set the sun, moon, and stars above;
You drove away darkness and gave us light;
You give us heat, cold and rain;
We receive them joyfully.

You created wind, water, fire, wild animals;
You succour birds and insects;
Grass, creepers, trees, berries, leaves, and flowers,
We look on them and are gladdened.

You have set the blue sea throughout the world.
Even though it was rough, you said 'Be calm!'
In it also you succour creatures.
You *are*! That we know of you!

Sung by the Kui people of the Kond hills of Orissa, India

289

O Lord, send us and our dusty neighbours around the world a good soaking of rain, about one and a half inches over the fifteen-hour period at a rate of no more than a tenth of an inch per hour, preferably at night; and repeat once a week until April 15, with the exception of the three weeks needed for spring planting; and thereafter once every two weeks until the soil-moisture deficit has been eliminated, or until the farmers wish it to stop, whichever comes first.

Nebraskan farmer

We meet such farmers in every land, though generally speaking his African and Asian counterparts are more philosophical about it, and more accepting when it does not work out as desired.

290

O heaven, send your rain in the fields!
My friend has sown seed and he is waiting for you.

Pushtu invocation, North-west frontier of Pakistan

291

O God, in whom we live, move and have our being, grant us the rain we need, so that your answer to our present earthly needs may give us greater confidence to ask for eternal benefits.

Roman liturgy

292

We pray, Lord, for the rising of the water of the Nile, this year. May Christ, our Saviour, bless it and raise it, cheering the earth and sustaining us, his creatures. And may the rising water remind us of the Living Water freely given to all who repent and believe.

Coptic Orthodox Liturgy, Egypt

293

O Lord, who art our guide
help us to accomplish speedily our wishes, and
fill with water our ships that have brought us
to such desperation.

Caravan Leader's Prayer

The invocation is sung by Bedouins when the caravans stop at watering places in the desert where the flow of water is poor. Watering the animals is a demanding and even hazardous task, for the animals are not always easy to handle, and in their rush to drink might well trample others to death. If twenty camels must slake their thirst at one of the poor water holes it may be necessary for as many as ten men to work for over four hours before they could attend to their own needs.

This makes the hassle over the weekend shopping and the rush at the check-out counter in the local supermarket, and the even more demanding care of domestic pets, seem a very light thing indeed. The constant supply of fresh water that we enjoy becomes a matter of profound thanksgiving.

294

Bless, O Lord, the plants, the vegetation, and the herbs of the field, that they may grow and increase to fullness and bear much fruit. And may the fruit of the land remind us of the spiritual fruit we should bear.

Coptic Orthodox Liturgy, Egypt

295

O God Above,
Make good for us all that we have cultivated.
Let it bear good fruit!
Let it be good fruit for us!
We shall eat new fruits –
green mangoes, ripe mangoes, mophua, dates –
Let them be for our whole well-being.
Deliver us from the tiger, the bear, the snake –
from all these venomous beasts;
Deliver us from all manner of disease;
from suffering unto death,
and from all our enemies.

Invocation used at the community eating of the first-fruits among the tribal people of the Kond hills of Orissa, India.

296

God of my needfulness, grant me
Something to eat, give me milk, give me
sons, give me herds, give me meat, O my Father.

African morning invocation

297

Lord Jesus Christ, Almighty, All-Generous and All-Merciful God, Who under the Old Dispensation didst miraculously feed Thy chosen people for forty years in the desert, and who in the time of famine didst, through Thy prophet Elijah, multiply the flour and oil of the widow at Zarephath, and under the New Dispensation didst feed five thousand with five loaves and four thousand with seven loaves, and Who in latter times didst work like miracles through the faith and prayers of Thy servants; look mercifully now, O Lord, upon us, Thy sinful servants, have mercy upon us and deliver us from the famine which threatens us; grant in Thine Omnipotence that we lack not the food we need, lest we untimely perish.

From a Russian *samizdat* typewritten book of prayers

298

O Lord who fed the multitudes with five barley loaves, bless what we are about to eat.

Arabic grace, Egypt

299

No ordinary meal – a sacrament awaits us
On our table spread.
For men are risking lives on sea and land
That we may dwell in safety and be fed.

Grace from Scotland

300

O Lord, our meal is steaming before us and it smells very good. The water is clear and fresh. We are happy and satisfied. But now we must think of our sisters and brothers all over the world who have nothing to eat and only a little to drink. Please, please through the help of their sisters and brothers, let them have enough to eat and enough to drink.

That is most important. But give them also what they need every day in order to get by. Amen.

Prayer from West Africa

301

In a somewhere-hungry, sometimes-lonely world, for this food and this company may we be truly thankful.

Christian Aid

302

God of our fathers
I am stretched out with no food,
I am stretched out with a raging stomach.
Others have taken food,
They are stretched out full;
Even if it is but a polecat,
Or a little rock rabbit,
I would be pleased with it.
I say the name of God
Father of my fathers.

Rolong tribe, South Africa

303

O thou Chief of Chiefs, we kneel before thee in obeisance and adoration. Like the bird in the branches we praise thy heavenly glory. Like the village sharpening stone, thou art always available and never exhausted. Remove, we pray thee, our sins that hide thy face. Thou knowest that we are poor and unlearned; that we often work when hungry. Send rain in due season for our gardens that our food may not fail. Protect us from the cold and danger by night. Help us to keep in health that we may rejoice in strength. May our villages be filled with children. Emancipate us from the fear of the fetish and the witch doctor and from all manner of superstitions. Save the people, especially the Christian boys

and girls in the villages, from the evil that surrounds them.
All this we ask in the name of Jesus Christ thy Son. Amen.

Prayer from Zaire

304

Ah, Lord, what! The weather is cold,
The fellest freeze that e'er I did feel.
I pray God help them that is old,
Or find it ill theyr limbs to wield.

Prayer of Joseph, York Mystery Plays, used by Help the Aged

305

O cold, cold, it is terribly cold –
There is no sunshine, my hands are icy cold,
O, this spell of cold!

The world looks cold to me.
My friends and my relations, they are all cold too.
My mind is gloomy –
Coldness is capturing my very soul.

Ha, still my heart beats,
And warm blood flows through my veins –
I rub my hands and I am warm again.

O world, cold friends,
In my constant struggle with you
I find warmth
And I can feel it.
You are not cold.
The coldness is in my thinking.

In the depth of my heart,
I feel the heat of the boiling love
Which my Lord has placed in me.
So warm is that love,
That it warms up my whole being,
And all seems warm to me.

O cold, where is your sting?
The love of my Lord has melted you away.

M. A. Thomas, India

306

Thank God for holy ice!

Prayer of Temple Gairdner during his last illness in Cairo

307

Bless, O God, bless my weatherbeaten soul.

Prayer of an old man, West Indies

308

. . . I am old now
They say I am going to die soon.
What a relief.
They tell me that I should go to the mission hospital, and
consult a doctor. The doctor examines me and he says I
have to take x-ray, injections and maybe operation.
I say, Doctor, how can I finance this?
He says, that is your problem, my hospital must become
self-supporting.
I went to a government hospital, after several visits they
examined me and gave me several prescriptions, but only
one red medicine all the time free of costs.
No relief so far.
Whether I survive or not, is not important anyway.

I was thinking what is next.
Thou need not worry about me, my Lord, I have tremendous capacity to suffer.

They tell me that I am bound to go to hell (if there is any)
because I was a sinner and a criminal throughout my life.
But as I have a tremendous capacity to suffer, maybe Thy
hell (if there is any) and judgement will be more humane

and comforting than the hell and judgement on the earth
created by Thy people.

I couldn't have done better than this.

We anxiously wait for Thy Kingdom to come on this earth.

My last prayer to Thee, O Lord, inspire, motivate and
convince Thy Government, Thy Society, Thy Church,
Thy good people, so that they can

'Love thy neighbour' in concrete terms by actions.

So they struggle with us in our suffering and struggle and
find hope in our hope, i.e. Thy hope.

It is high time my Lord.

I have finished my Lord.

I am ready for your mercy or for your judgement. Amen.

> Sudhakar S. Ramteke, India. A poor man's Nunc Dimittis.

309

Day ends:
Breasting the North
My shoulders shiver
As I onward go.
And yet,
I utterly forget
The cruel cold,
Nor feel the dark,
Because my heart
Aches with the people's woe.
Oh, let me trust
That through my tears
God's kingdom has
One little inch drawn near!

Then what is it to me
That my weak body be
Beaten to dust?
Midnight;
I crawl from my bed
Into the cold,

And gaze at the stars again,

Finding God there
To help me bear
My daily load
Of grief and care,
Sorrow and pain.

Deep in the night
Our spirits meet,
And prayer is sweet!

Toyohiko Kagawa, 1888–1960, Japan

310

I'm tired, God. But I'll lift one foot if you'll lift the other
for me.

Saidie Patterson, Shankhill, Northern Ireland

311

Thou has led me through my crowded travels of the day to
my evening's loneliness.
I wait for its meaning through the stillness of the night.

Rabindranath Tagore: Evening prayer

312

Father, we pray for all lonely people, especially those who,
coming home to an empty house, stand at the door hesitant
and afraid to enter. May all who stand in any doorway with
fear in their hearts, like the two on the Emmaus Road, ask
the Living One in. Then, by his grace, may they find that in
loneliness they are never alone, and that he peoples empty
rooms with his presence.

E. M. Farr

Sorrowing over the death of his wife, Kathleen, E. M.
Blaiklock uses this Emmaus-based prayer

313

O Lord, be gracious unto us! In all that we hear or see, in all that we say or do, be gracious unto us. I ask pardon of the Great God. I ask pardon at the sunset, when every sinner turns to Him. Now and forever I ask pardon of God. O Lord, cover us from our sins, guard our children and protect our weaker friends.

Camel driver's prayer

314

'Jesus has turned our sunsets into sunrises' – or so the saying goes.

Jesus, may this be so not only for me, but for all like me, who are fearful and apprehensive of endings of any kind.

Help us to live and end our days in the faith and fear of your resurrection.

JBC

315

Praise God who sends us the light of heaven.

Prayer commonly used in homes in India at the lighting of the lamps.

316

Christ is the Light of our souls:
We rejoice in this Light, great source of truth.
Christ is the Light of our homes:
We rejoice in this Light, great source of peace.
Christ is the Light of the world:
We rejoice in this Light, great source of hope.
Go out as Christ's true lights; disperse the darkness of evil;
For his grace, his power, his peace go with you.

Prayer used at the ceremony of Lighting of Lamps at the Andhra Christian Theological College, Hyderabad, India

As thou hast set the moon in the sky to be the poor man's lantern, so let thy light shine in my dark life and lighten my path; as the rice is sown in the water and brings forth grain in great abundance, so let thy word be sown in our midst that the harvest may be great; and as the banyan sends forth its branches to take root in the soil, so let thy life take root in our lives.

Prayer from India

We thank thee, God, for the moments of fulfilment:
    the end of a day's work,
    the harvest of sugar cane,
    the birth of a child,
for in these pauses, we feel the rhythm of the eternal. Amen.

Prayer from Hawaii

Lord, may I be wakeful at sunrise to begin a new day for Thee, cheerful at sunset for having done my work for Thee; thankful at moonrise and under starshine for the beauty of Thy universe. And may I add what little may be in me to add to Thy great world.

The Abbot of Greve

320

Blessed art thou, O Lord our God, King of the universe,
Who at thy word bringest on the evening twilight.

With wisdom openest the gates of the heavens,
And with understanding changest times and variest
   seasons,
And arrangest the stars in their watches in the sky,
According to thy will.

Thou createst day and night;
Thou rollest away the light from before the darkness,
And the darkness from before the light;
Thou makest the day to pass and the night to approach,
And dividest the day from the night.

The Lord of hosts is thy name;
A God living and enduring continually,
Mayest thou reign over us for ever and ever.
Blessed art thou, O Lord, who bringest on the evening
   twilight.

Jewish prayer

321

We pray thee, O Creator of every thing, at this hour preced-
ing night, that thou be clement and watch over us.

Let dreams and phantoms of the night be scattered. Keep
us safe from our enemy and make us pure!

Attributed to St Ambrose of Milan, 340–397

When she had prayed the evening prayer, she said: O my God, in kings' palaces the doors are closed, the curtains drawn. Every lover is alone with his beloved. Here is my station, between Thy hands.

Sufi recollection of God's closeness as night draws near

323

Dear Jesus, as a hen covers her chicks with her wings to keep them safe, do thou this dark night protect us under your golden wings.

Prayer from India

324

Come, oh Father, here I am: let us go on.
I know that my words are those of a child;
but it is *Thy* child that prays to Thee. It
is *Thy* dark I walk in, it is *Thy* hand I hold.

George MacDonald in *Castle Warlock*

325

God in Heaven, you have helped my life to grow like a tree. Now something has happened. Satan, like a bird, has carried in one twig of his own choosing after another. Before I knew it he had built a dwelling place and was living in it. Tonight, my Father, I am throwing out both the bird and the nest. Amen

Nigerian Christian

326

Come, Lord, and cover me with the night. Spread your grace over us as you assured us you would do.
Your promises are more than all the stars in the sky;
Your mercy is deeper than the night.
Lord, it will be cold.

The night comes with its breath of death.
Night comes, the end comes,
but Jesus Christ comes also.
Lord, we wait for him day and night.

Prayer from West Africa

327

Man is but small in the presence of God!
He is small when he stands up,
small when he walks,
small when he works,
for then the world is greater than he.
But man is great when he lies down,
for then his spirit rises
unto unknown worlds,
rises towards heaven.
Our life is a book of mystery
written by God, mysterious and all-powerful;
and only in sleep is it given
to search through the pages of his book!
Sleep, sleep, sleep,
Sleep is close to death,
and death is close to God.

Algerian prayer

328

Lord, give to every man his own death –
the dying that grows out of that life
wherein he had love and sense and plight.

Jean Marie Rilke

329

You were my death;
You I could hold
when all fell away from me.

Jewish prayer

Lord, I thank Thee for night,
the time of cool and quiet,
the time of sweet enchantment
when a deep mystery pervades everything.
The time when soul speaks to soul in common desire
to partake of the hush of the ineffable.
The time when the moon and the stars
speak to man of his high calling and destiny.
The time of repose and calm
when the fever of the mind subsides
and uncertainty gives place
to the sense of eternal purpose.
O Lord, I thank Thee for night.

> Chandran Devanesen, India: night prayer

Father, as downland pond,
Fed by the visiting dews
Which every night respond
To what the days diffuse,

So, through the dark's deface,
Pooled may my spirit be;
Alembic of thy grace,
Thy love's distillery.

Thomas Browne, 1605–82: An Evening Colloquy with God

In the name of the Lord God of Israel, may Michael, the
protection of God, be at my right hand; and Gabriel, the
power of God, at my left; before me Uriel, the light of God;
behind me Raphael, the healing of God; and above my head
Shechinat El, the presence of God.

> Hebrew night prayer for children

333

Save us O Lord waking; guard us sleeping;
That awake we may watch with Christ,
   and asleep we may rest in peace.

Compline: Antiphon to Nunc Dimittis

334

To God be glory;
To the angels honour;
To Satan confusion;
To the Cross reverence;
To the Church exaltation;
To the departed quickening;
To the penitent acceptance;
To the sick and infirm recovery and healing;
And to the four quarters of the world great peace and
   tranquillity;
And on us who are weak and sinful may the compassion
   and mercies of our God come, and may they
   overshadow us continually.   Amen.

Prayer from the old Syriac, used by Christians in Turkey, Persia,
and South India

335

As the earth keeps turning, hurtling through space, and
   night falls and day breaks from land to land,
Let us remember people – waking, sleeping, being born,
   and dying – one world, one humanity.
Let us go from here in peace.

Prayer used at the 6th WCC Assembly, Vancouver

Bye-bye, sun . . .

'It is the nights in prison which are the most difficult to bear, the long nights from lights-out until 5.30 the next morning,' wrote Ruth First in *An Account of Confinement under the South African 90 Day Detention Law*. And from personal experience she told how, after days and nights of interrogation, her captors resorted to the refined cruelty of releasing her to go home to her children, immediately re-arresting her again outside the prison gates, pushing her back into its darkness once more with the repeated taunt: 'Bye-bye sun, Bye-bye, sun.'*

'Bye-bye, sun', it seems to me, would be a very fitting way of describing that familiar Collect which concludes the Order of Evening Prayer in the Book of Common Prayer and certainly one which affirms the prayer's relevance to the dark places of the world.

> Lighten our darkness, we beseech Thee, O Lord: and by Thy great mercy defend us from all perils and dangers of this night.

First discovered and added to his collection of prayers by an early pope, Gelasius, somewhere around the year 492, the collect was one of a number of prayers prayed at an even earlier date; enabling us to feel what Italian churchmen felt in the latter half of the fifth century, when fear of enemies was widespread, and savage barbarians hammering on the doors of Rome made prayer for deliverance seem natural and urgent.

And undoubtedly such prayers as this, picked up on hazardous journeys, seemed very well suited to the needs of

---

*Ruth First was killed in Maputo in August 1982 by a South African letter bomb.

the early missionaries to these islands, crossing unknown seas and faced with our benighted heathen forefathers.

'Which liturgy shall be used, that of Gaul or that of Rome?' asked Augustine, writing back to Gregory from Britain at the close of the sixth century. 'It is my pleasure,' replied Gregory, 'that if thou hast found anything which would better please Almighty God, either in the Roman or in the Gallican or in any other Church, *that* thou shouldest teach in the Church of the Angles, which is as yet new in the faith. (For things are not to be loved for the sake of place, but places for the sake of good things.) Select therefore from each Church those things that are pious, religious, and rightful, and when thou has collected them into a whole, instill them in the minds of the Angles for their use . . .'

And so he did; and among 'those things', was the prayer 'Lighten our darkness . . .' which has proved to be 'pious, religious and rightful' to countless generations of Christians, regardless of place.

It was not, however, until nearly ten centuries later, and as a result of the work of Thomas Cranmer, expanding, paraphrasing and translating the collects into his incomparable English, and re-ordering the monastic offices into something resembling the people's services of Morning and Evening Prayer, that such prayers were really 'instilled into the minds of the Angles, for their use'. And in spite of the fact that they didn't make as much use of them as Cranmer would have hoped for and wished, it is probably true to say that Evensong, though often stayed-away from, has held a place in the affections of Angles, unequalled by any other service, to this very night.

The story is told of how during the Second World War, a crippled British bomber was trying to get back to England from a raid over Germany. Lights were out in the aircraft and the plane was in distress. The crew gave the 'mayday' signal which was received by the British base, but as the signal was being used as a hoax by enemy aircraft, the base refused to take action and the airfield lights remained off.

The men in the plane were desperate. 'We must have light' said one. 'Why not try praying' said another. And so it was that that collect learned by one of them in school, and long since fallen into disuse, was brought into service again, and repeated from memory. It was picked up on the radio at the base far below: 'Lighten our darkness, we beseech Thee O Lord, and by Thy great mercy defend us from all perils and dangers of this night.' 'That's not the enemy' said the men on the ground. 'Put on all lights . . .'

But this prayer is more than password and proof of Englishness; for when, nearly two centuries ago, the turn of our forefathers came to cross the dark seas and to take the Gospel to other lands, British missionaries to Africa and Asia carried with them Cranmer's book in full assurance that Cranmer's language would suffice, or at least prove translatable; so that prayers which, in the much-quoted phrase of Lord Macaulay, had already soothed the griefs of forty generations of Christians, might continue their good work in even darker places.

There is a comfort and relevance about the words of this collect which it is difficult to equal. At our best, as Christians of whatever nationality or generation, we go out in the spirit, and within the total concern, of a prayer such as this, to preach a gospel, and to be a presence which is designed to soothe the grief of our fellow human beings.

In one part of the world the prayer's relevance was stumbled upon by a missionary in Sierra Leone who confessed to having spent years of his ministry in remote villages fruitlessly talking about salvation from sin, only to discover that his people's greatest need was freedom from fear of the powers of darkness; while in Iran the words of this prayer were adapted for the main Sunday evening service with the addition of the one word 'specially'. 'Specially this night,' they prayed, conveying the sense both of immediacy and impermanence felt by Persian Christians to the present time.

In South India a bishop suggested that in his area 'maybe the drinking of illicit liquor and all the misery this brings, is one of the perils from which people ought to pray to be preserved,' and confessed that this need was certainly in his mind as he used the collect in that setting. In another part of the Indian subcontinent a little group of Bengali nuns in Bangladesh pray each evening 'Lighten our darkness . . . O Lord,' adding with delightful simplicity, 'But please do something about the world energy crisis, for the cobras here are so enjoying the darkness.'

The adaptations range to the insecurity and anxiety felt by Christians in Bible lands east and west of Jordan, once hallowed by our Lord's physical presence, to whom Arab Christians continue to refer even today as 'the One who walks by night'. During the civil war in 1970, huddled together in family bathrooms, it was to this 'One who walks by night' that they addressed psalms and prayers, display-ing – so an eye witness reports – the most astonishing trust in God's ability to protect them from bomb and bullet. 'I can well remember,' writes that same witness to those sad events, 'the first night I was in Jerusalem twenty-two years previously, and the shooting as the Mandate was drawing to a close, and walking to St George's Cathedral for Even-song, and hearing that prayer. And', she adds, 'so many times in later years I have continued to pray it with an intensity born of that experience.'

Those words 'so many times' and 'with . . . intensity' seem to me to be important words. For they give the lie to the idea that there may be some magic about any pattern of words, but suggest rather that, used regularly and meaning-fully, this is a prayer which somehow gradually reaches down into the depths of a person's being and becomes part of that person as against the day when some special kind of response will be called for.

That day came some years later for a misionary couple with children in Yahya Khan's Pakistan, who were suddenly faced with the question as to whether evacuation was the best means for their defence against all the perils and dangers confronting them at that time. They decided against it, 'Steadied,' as they wrote at the time, 'by the stuff of which "Lighten our darkness" is made.'

Becoming 'the stuff of which "Lighten our darkness" is made', is, I suppose, one of the objects of saying a prayer such as this, regularly and with intensity, allowing it to become part of us, and we a part of it.

As it happened, at the same time as that decision was being reached in Pakistan; across the border in India, the country with which Pakistan was at war, another missionary, travelling in a blacked-out train, was also praying that prayer. 'At night,' she wrote, 'we travelled in total darkness, with shutters down and only a candle stump to cheer us up. But for me at this time that prayer was answered *quite literally*, in the person of the Indian woman fellow-traveller who gave me a candle; in the care of the Hindu guard who went up and down the carriages all night long to see to our safety; arriving in Delhi station, also in the complete dark, in the coolie who carried my luggage to a taxi; and in the taxi driver carrying on with his job through unlit streets.' 'And', she added, 'not *one* of them knew that what they did was "for the love of God's only Son" but each was certainly contributing to the protection of at least one grateful traveller, "from all the perils and dangers" of that particular night.'

Which in itself only serves to underline one further very important aspect of our use of this prayer. It is clearly a prayer for which *we ourselves* must provide part of the answer; by gratefully acknowledging our solidarity with those who, of whatever opinion or cause or faith, are seeking to eradicate the perils and dangers surrounding God's children throughout the world, striving against every kind of fear that men may take to bed with them; and working for the day when *no* human being anywhere may ever be able to say to another human being, 'Bye-bye, sun.'

Lighten our darkness,
Lord, we pray;
and in your mercy defend us
from all perils and dangers of this night;
for the love of your only Son,
our Saviour Jesus Christ.

The Alternative Service Book

Some years ago I was in the Kathmandu Valley in Nepal, and was walking with a Christian doctor down the long and narrow main street of the small old city state of Paten. The street was dark with overhanging houses decorated with beautiful Newar wood carvings. In the centre of the town there was the usual conglomeration of what I felt to be rather oppressive temples, most of them in a rather bad state of repair, and very dirty, with dogs fighting among the gods, children defecating wherever they pleased, rats rumaging in the piles of rubbish. And yet in the midst of this seeming casualness and disregard, the frequent sound of bells indicated that some kind of worship was going on, and garlands of freshly collected marigolds, pathetic, messy little piles of food, small guttering lights, fresh fat glistening on the grotesque gods themselves, all indicated something profoundly, disturbingly, un-cerebral, in the presence of which, I confess, I felt completely out of my depth.

Faces peered out of dark window frames as in the dusk we made our way out of Paten; and as we walked a small boy wearing a rather grubby shirt and with a very dirty nose, rushed out and clutched my companion's skirt. She obviously knew him. His father and mother, she explained, had become Christians in some other part of Nepal; had been baptized and then imprisoned. And finally, under pressure, had recanted and had come back and lost themselves in the life of this Newar town. The wife, apparently, still came occasionally, to the small Christian service, but seemed to be losing heart, for the darkness and the drag and the deviousness of this city, and the demands of her young family, were all pulling in the opposite direction.

I don't know what kind of Christian instruction that boy's mother and father, those short-time Christians, had received. They certainly would not have heard of a prayer book published in 1662 when their Newar city was at the height of its glory, nor would they ever have heard of the almost flawless, sophisticated liturgical service called Evening Prayer; but if they had, I thought to myself, they would have found in it that totally appropriate prayer, which I felt exactly suited their needs and also my own, and which – on all our behalfs – I said quietly to myself as in the semi-darkness we walked out of the city of Paten.

> Lighten our darkness, we beseech Thee, O Lord; and by Thy great mercy defend us from all perils and dangers of this night.

And in praying it thus, and in that setting, I felt I had done a better job than had I prayed it at a thousand polite Anglican evensongs. But then, perhaps one of the reasons why the Third Collect is placed in Evensong, is to prevent us getting too polite, to remind us that the closing of day and the falling of darkness is a time not for relaxing the grip, but a time of increased Christian responsibility; is a time to be kept through and in Jesus Christ our Lord, caring and praying for those who cry out in any kind of fear in the dark, sore, lonesome, inarticulate places of the world, our own hearts included.

Sources and acknowledgements

Where the exact source of a prayer is unknown or self-evident, no specific acknowledgements have been made below. All other prayers and meditations are gratefully (and I hope correctly) acknowledged.

Allen and Unwin, London, Martin Lings, *Twentieth Century Sufi Saints of Tunisia*, 36 Amnesty International, 251 Andhra Christian Theological College, Hyderabad, 164 (slightly adapted), 317.

Bishop's College, Calcutta, *The Priest's Book of Private Prayers*, 52 *Book of Common Prayer*, 46 and pp. 136, 142. Extracts from the Book of Common Prayer, which is Crown Copyright in the United Kingdom, are reproduced by permission of Eyre, & Spottiswoode (Publishers) Limited, Her Majesty's Printers, London.

Jonathan Cape, London, Etty Hillesam *Etty, A Diary 1941–43* (trs. Arnold J. Pomerans), 111 Caribbean Conference of Churches, N. Dexter and P. Jordan, *Sing a New Song*, 286 Central Board of Finance of the Church of England, *The Alternative Service Book* 1980, pp. 1, 141 The Leonard Cheshire Foundation, 255 Christian Aid, 96, 140, 182, 301 The Christian Literature Society of India, Barbara Boal, *The Fire is Easy*, 288, 295; A Seeker, *A Kind of Seeking*, 71, 141; M. A. Thomas, *About You and Me*, 173, 193, 233, 268, 281 Church Missionary Society, London, 19, 23, 74, 161, 185, 218, 239; Subir Biswas, *Lord, Let Me Share*, 145, 174, 215, 275 Church Pastoral Aid Society, London, Dick Williams (ed.) *Prayers for Today's Church*, 253 William Collins/Fontana, London, George Appleton, *Journey for a Soul*, 72 Community of the Resurrection, Mirfield, 223 and 252 (quoted in Fr Jonathan Graham, *Mirfield Essays*) Doris Compton *Whisper in the Pines: a collection of verses from Ishmael*, privately printed, 3 Congregational World Mission, 158 Coptic Orthodox Patriarchate, Cairo, 55, 292, 294 Corrymeela Community, Belfast, 112   Bishop Kenneth Cragg, *A Calendar of Middle East Saints*, 205, 241.

Darton, Longman and Todd, London, Metropolitan Anthony, *Courage to Prayer* (quoting Sud Deutsche Zeitung), 252; Michael Bourdeaux, *Risen Indeed: lessons in faith from the USSR*, 45, 58, 61; Dom Helder Camara, *A Thousand Reasons for Living*, 43, 70, 198, 262, 272; Donald Nicholl, *Holiness*, 31   Diocese of Calcutta, *Arati* (Diocesan Newsletter), 154, 156; Litany, 270   Diocese of Southwark, Ivor Smith-Cameron, *Pilgrimage*, 271   Durgapur Industrial Service, India, 308   E. J. Dwyer, Johann Hoffman-Herreros, *Your Hand, God: praying with children*, 225.

El Al Israel Airlines Ltd., 93   Faber and Faber, London, Dag Hammarskjöld, *Markings* (trs. W. H. Auden and Leif Sjoberg), 279   Forward Movement Publications, Cincinnati, *Anglican Cycle of Prayer*; *Partners in Prayer*, 117, 152, 203, 287   Friendship Press, New York, Chandran Devanesen, *The Cross is Lifted*, 8, 73, 176, 266, 330; Fritz Pawelzik, *I Lie on My Mat and Pray: prayers by young African Christians*, 57, 100, 216; Fritz Pawelzik, *I Sing Your Praise All Day Long*, 133, 327; Bless Wiant, *Worship Resources from the Chinese*, 139   Frontier magazine, 207.

Gill and Macmillan, Dublin, Michael Quoist, *Prayers of Life*, 190.

Harper and Row, San Francisco, D. J. Fleming, *The World at One in Prayer*, 4, 9, 10, 15, 38, 48, 87, 108, 113, 175, 183, 226, 227, 231, 237, 303, 323, 325   William Heinemann, London, Chinua Achebe, *No Longer at Ease*. 13 (Copyright © 1960 by Chinua Achebe, and reprinted by permission of the publishers.); Alfonso M. di Nola, *The Prayers of Man, from Primitive Peoples to Present Times*, 88, 89, 265, 291, 293, 327   Hodder and Stoughton, Sevenoaks, E. M. Blaiklock, *Kathleen* (quoting E. M. Farr), 312; Mary Craig, *Blessings*, 184; Viktor Frankl, *Man's Search for Meaning*, 30; Cecil Hunt, *Uncommon Prayers for Younger People*, 11, 56, 293, 299   Holy Land, Summer 1983, Jerusalem, 35.

Jerusalem and Middle East Church Association, 155.

Keston College, Bromley, 104, 132, 180, 249, 297   John Knox Press, Atlanta, Kazoh Katamori, *The Theology of the Pain of God*,

1; Richard Wong, *Prayers from an Island*, 25, 163, 177, 210, 212, 238, 282, 318.

Latin American Women's Ecumenical Council, *Agenda 1979*, 170   Lutheran World Federation, *Children in Conversation with God*, 225.

Macmillan, London, Rabindranath Tagore, *Collected Poems and Plays*, 'Stray Birds', 5, 51, 136, 142, 160, 167, 285, 311; Gitanjali, xxxix, 68; Gitanjali xlv, 65 (used by permission of the Trustees and Macmillan, London and Basingstoke)   Mr Randle Manwaring, 206   Methodist Church Overseas Division, *Now* magazine, 274 (from *Cartas A Jesus*, trs. Sarah Bysouth); *Prayer Manual*, 26, 147, 148, 159

Orbis Books, Maryknoll, NY, Walbert Buhlman, *The Coming of the Third Church*, 261   Oxford University Press, Eric Milner-White and G. W. Briggs, *Daily Prayer*, 114.

Paternoster Press, Exeter, J. E. Church, *Quest for the Highest: a diary of the East African Revival*, 82, 135   Pax Christi, 248   Peter Pauper Press, New York, 313   Les Presses de Taizé, *La Prière Oecuménique*, 41 (translated and adapted)   Province of Central Africa, *Epifania* (Newsletter), 157.

Routledge and Kegan Paul, London, A Nicholson Reynand, *The Mystics of Islam*, 33.

Rev Michael Saward, *Task Unfinished*, 243   SCM Press, London, Florence Allshorn, *Notebooks*, 29; William W. Simpson, *Jewish Prayer and Worship*, 144; M. A. Thomas, *Meditations of an Indian Christian*, 54, 90, 305; Ken Walsh, *Sometimes I Weep*, 110   Sheldon Press, London, Kenneth Cragg, *The Wisdom of the Sufis*, 11, 16, 17, 21, 40, 49, 143, 322   Society for Promoting Christian Knowledge, London, George Appleton, *Jerusalem Prayers for the World Today*, 64; George Appleton, *One Man's Prayers*, 64, 247, 284; John Mbiti, *The Prayers of African Religion*, 296; Constance Padwick, *Muslim Devotions*, 79; J. S. Purvis (ed.) *The York Cycle of Mystery Plays* 304; Kathryn Spink (ed.) *In the Silence of the Heart: Meditations by Mother Teresa of Calcutta and her co-workers*, 60, 81, 200, 276, 283   St Albans Cathedral, Pretoria, *The Sword*, 256, 269.

United Church of Pakistan, *Lahore Diocesan Leaflet*, 131   United Society for the Propagation of the Gospel, London, 38, 85, 138; *Network*, 27 (quoted from *Berita*, Seminari Theoloji, Malaysia), 115, 157; *Prayers for Mission*, 14, 109, 147, 307   University Book Agency, Peshawar, 290 (trs. Jens Enevoldsen)   The Upper Room, Nashville, Robert H. Adams, Jr., *A Traveller's Prayer Book*, 235 (adapted).

Week of Prayer for World Peace, 194, 236, 265   World Council of Churches, Geneva, *Community of Women and Men in Church Study*, 172; *For All God's People*, 41 (from Les Presses de Taizé, see above), 232, 242, 261; *Jesus Christ the Light of the World*, 6th WCC World Assembly, Vancouver 1983, 178, 179, 217, 221 (also 41st Eucharistic Congress, Philadelphia 1976), 254; *Risk*, Vol. II nos. 2 and 3, 335   World Student Christian Federation, Geneva, *Venite Adoremus II*, 208, 214.

Exact sources unknown 6, 18, 37, 47, 50, 53, 63, 66, 67, 69, 75, 77, 78, 86, 103, 105, 106, 107, 123, 134, 146, 150, 151, 169, 170, 187, 189, 197, 199, 204, 213, 225, 229, 230, 240, 277, 278, 289, 298, 299, 302, 306, 317, 335.